On a Wing
and a
Prayer

On a Wing
and a
Prayer

KATHERINE VALENTINE

IMAGE BOOKS   DOUBLEDAY

New York   London   Toronto   Sydney   Auckland

AN IMAGE BOOK
PUBLISHED BY DOUBLEDAY
a division of Random House, Inc.

IMAGE, DOUBLEDAY, and the portrayal of a deer drinking from a stream
are registered trademarks of Random House, Inc.

Book design by Elizabeth Rendfleisch

Library of Congress Cataloging-in-Publication Data
Valentine, Katherine.
On a wing and a prayer / Katherine Valentine.— 1st ed.
p. cm.
1. New England—Social life and customs—Fiction.
2. City and town life—Fiction. I. Title.
PS3622.A44O5 2005
813'.6—dc22
2005042045

ISBN 0-385-51201-5

PRINTED IN THE UNITED STATES OF AMERICA

August 2005

First Edition

1 3 5 7 9 10 8 6 4 2

To my patron, Saint Anthony,
who has watched over me since I was a child.
May others find comfort in your prayers.

ACKNOWLEDGMENTS

The inspiration for this novel came from a story a priest friend shared concerning his near drowning as a child.

Having gone skating on an ice-covered harbor, he ventured out too far and plunged into the water. Panic began to set in as he realized that, trapped beneath a thick covering of ice, he was drowning. Just when he was about to give up all hope, he heard the voice of his mother, who had recently died, calling to him, "Come this way." Somehow, he managed to follow the voice, which led to an opening. There, eager hands reached out and pulled him to safety.

As with all works of fiction, when authors tackle a new subject, they must rely on the expertise of others. In that vein, I wish to thank Chief Lewis R. Clark of the Morris Fire Department for helping me to understand the complexities of an ice-related drowning, especially that of a child. He generously provided me with access to equipment, answered endless questions about procedures, and even invited me to be present the next time the department took the iceboat out to practice retrieval of a drowning victim. (I graciously declined.)

Thanks to state trooper Sergeant Grey Kenney, assigned to the Litchfield, Connecticut, barracks, for his help in deciphering police protocol and issues concerning the state police Dive Team.

Once again, kudos to the Doubleday editorial staff—Michelle Rapkin, my delightful editor and beloved friend, whose gentle guidance always makes for a better book, and to her assistant, Jennifer Kim, for overseeing the myriad details. A round of applause is also due to my agent, Amy Berkower, who works tirelessly on my behalf. Thank you for continuing to believe in the dream.

Most important, thanks to my dear husband and in-house editor, "Saint Paul," for reading countless revisions, each with equal enthusiasm. *Now that the book is done, how about that vacation?*

On a Wing
——— and a ———
Prayer

Chapter One

The night was dark as pitch, the moon and stars erased by a thick cloud cover that gave those wandering outdoors the feeling that they were in the midst of a cavernous mine.

It was after nine o'clock, considered late by most Dorsetville standards. Still, the members of Saint Cecilia's parish council lingered, attributable to both Mrs. Norris's apple-cranberry pie and the icy patches that only hours ago had been soft pools of water under the March thaw. Folks huddled over hot cups of coffee, reluctant to brave the brisk wind, the icy interiors of their cars, or the dark drive home.

Father James watched George Benson cut his fourth wedge of pie and a slice of Vermont cheddar. At this rate, there wouldn't be any leftovers, a problem he had never encountered before George was elected to the parish council.

"Pass the cream," George said, refilling his coffee mug.

Harry Clifford had brought a large thermos of coffee from the Country Kettle. This, too, George had nearly depleted. Father James passed the cream and harnessed a growing sense of resentment.

George wolfed down a sizable wedge of cheese, licked his fingers, then belched. His manners were about as uncouth as his appearance—greasy overalls, oil-stained fingers. This newest council member owned a heating and air-conditioning business and didn't feel it necessary to wash or change for meetings, which accounted for the strategic seating arrangements. George sat alone on one side of the ten-foot table. Ethel Johnson, Harriet Bedford, Sam Rosenberg (who had driven Harriet), Mary Pritchett, Harry Clifford, Mike Gallagher, and Father James were crowded along the opposite side. Ethel's golden retriever, Honey, lay underneath.

"I heard that you and your wife have been looking to buy some real estate down south," George told Harry Clifford, scraping the last bit of pastry off his plate with his thumb.

"How'd you hear that?" Harry wanted to know.

"Esther Fitzsimons told me. I was fixing her toilet the other day. You wouldn't believe what was stuffed down there. It looked like—"

"George!" Father James interrupted forcefully. "We really don't need to know the details."

"Are you and Nellie thinking about buying a vacation home?" Harriet asked.

"We considered it."

"They're moving down there. Permanently. They're retiring," George stated emphatically.

"Retiring?" Father James said with a gasp, splashing coffee down the front of his shirt.

"Now wait a minute—" Harry began.

"That's what Esther told me," George said, plowing right over Harry's protestations. "She said that Nellie came into school last week complaining about the cold and said that they were moving someplace warm."

"Moving?" Ethel said, sinking back in her chair. Honey, sensing something was deeply wrong, leaned heavily against her lap.

For several seconds folks sat in stunned silence. Harry's retirement had never occurred to any of them. Harry owned the Country Kettle, and Dorsetville without the Country Kettle was . . . well . . . unimaginable.

Where would Mike Gallagher take his ten-year-old twin boys for malteds after their hockey games; or Father James go for home fries, golden brown with crispy laced edges; or the seniors for their morning toast and coffee after mass?

"Now, listen everyone. Nellie and I have no intention—" Harry began, trying to set things straight, but George cut him off.

"That's not what Esther said," George piped in, leaning back in his chair. "She said Nellie told her that you were moving."

Harry shook his head in exasperation. "We are *not* moving, George."

"Then why would Esther say you were?"

"I don't know. Maybe Nellie mentioned that we had been talking about it . . . ," he said, hedging.

"See, I told you!" George smiled, feeling he had been vindicated.

"You know how it is this time of year," Harry explained. "By mid-March, we've all had enough of the ice and snow. Nellie and I just got up one morning last week and starting talking about how nice it would be to live someplace where you didn't have to tunnel your way out to the car each morning. But that's all it was. Honest. Just talk."

Everyone gave a collective sigh of relief. Everyone, that is, except George.

"You know, it's not half a bad idea for you two to start thinking about retiring." George was like a dog with a bone. He was not letting this go. "You're no spring chickens anymore."

Retirement? Why the devil would George want to put that idea in Harry's head? Father James wondered. Blast the man! He ran a finger around his collar, which suddenly seemed rather tight.

"Nellie and I just turned fifty," Harry said, a little put off. "We've got a few years left before we reach our 'golden years.' "

Father James relaxed.

"I think you're foolish. Why, if I had your kind of money, come the first snowfall, I'd be on a plane to the Bahamas."

"You make us sound as though our middle name is Midas."

"You got a restaurant, a bakery, plus Nellie's salary. I'd say you're doing pretty well."

"Now listen here, George. Our finances are not up for discussion."

"You can't take it with you, Harry," George said sagely. "You might as well spend it if you got it, so why not spend it wintering in a place where it's warm? Why, just look at the weather tonight. It's cold enough to freeze the tits off Platt's cows."

"George Benson!" Harriet chastised. "Mind your manners. You're in the basement of Lord's house."

"What did I say?" he asked with absolute innocence.

Mary Pritchett could see that a change in subject matter was desperately needed and so she offered, "Wasn't the weather lovely last weekend?"

"Felt almost like spring," Father James quickly answered, happy to get away from all the talk about Harry retiring or wintering down south. If he ever discovered who had voted George Benson onto the parish council, he might strongly suggest they seek absolution.

"I took my Girl Scout troop on a field trip over to Fenn's Pond," Mary continued. "The crocus is in bloom. They're just lovely."

Harriet, who owned the local nursery, had donated a hundred bulbs last fall to the Garden Club's annual beautification project.

"I heard one of the girls fell in," Ethel chuckled.

Mary rolled her eyes. "That would be Leah Kilbourne. I told her to stay off the ice, but Leah had to test it out. Luckily, she fell in at the edge, not in the deep end."

"Speaking of water," George interjected. "Did anyone notice the large water stain behind Saint Anthony's statue?"

"I was going to ask you about that," Father James said.

"It's coming from the pipe chase that runs down behind the wall," George explained. Taking a checkered handkerchief from his back pocket, he blew his nose, gave it a hard swipe, and stuffed the handkerchief back into his pants pocket, then concluded, "In order to fix it, that back section of the wall will have to be torn down. It's the only way I can get to the leak."

"How long will it take to repair?" asked Harry, who was president of the parish council.

"Depends on what I find," George said, pushing back his chair. "Now, if no one is going to eat this last piece of pie, I think I'll finish it off."

The meeting broke up a little after ten o'clock. Deputy Hill watched from across the street as council members navigated their way along the icy asphalt pathway under Father James's admonitions to be careful.

He buried his hands inside his thermo-lined jacket and shivered, figuring that if he made it through tonight's shift without getting frostbite, it would be a miracle.

The row of arched streetlamps cast small pools of yellow light onto the sidewalks, revealing patches of ice and crusted snow. He glanced over at the large wrought-iron clock stationed near the entryway to the town park and felt his heart sink. There were still two and a half hours to go.

Stuffing his hands deeper into his pockets, he plodded on. His hopes of ever restoring his place with the sheriff were as empty as the starless sky. Night patrol was his punishment for having totaled the department's new police cruiser and taking Sam Rosenberg's Plymouth Duster along with it. Fortunately for Sam, a group of friends had restored his car; however, Hill doubted if anyone could restore his standing with the sheriff. This was the third vehicle that had met its demise while under his care.

A tabby cat dashed out from behind a cluster of bushes and crossed the street. Hill watched it disappear beneath Valerie Kilbourne's front porch. Poor thing, out on a night like this, he thought. Maybe he should knock on a few doors and try to find out where it belonged. Just then Valerie stuck her head out the front door and called, "Rufus." The cat leaped onto the porch and disappeared like liquid mercury through the open doorway.

Hill stamped his feet, which had frozen into solid blocks of ice, as a sharp wind lashed across his face, adding to his discomfort. If he didn't find a place to get warm soon, he'd die from hypothermia. He searched the quiet avenue for a light, someone who might invite him in for a hot cup of cocoa, and perhaps a word or two of sympathy, but it seemed as though everyone had gone to bed. The homes on the west side of the street slumbered quietly, and directly across the avenue, Saint Cecilia's rectory now lay quiet. Even the porch light had been turned off. Of course, he could always go back to the station and warm up, but he didn't want to risk being accused of shirking his patrol. He was in enough trouble. Better to stay out here and freeze.

For just a moment Hill felt a strange sense of foreboding, and he quickly tried to assess its origins. To the natural eye, the lane appeared quiet, yet he felt an undercurrent of movement in the air, a feeling of expectancy as though beneath the cover of darkness something had begun to stir to life. A sliver of fear snaked its way up his spine. He wasn't accustomed to these kinds of fanciful thoughts, and he tried to shake them off as a dog would water from a swim in the pond. Still, they lingered.

Then his eyes came to rest on Saint Cecilia's Church, a misshapen mass of stone and mortar of indiscernible architectural style, sitting like a paperweight on the northern side of the green. A small orb of light flickered, reflecting through a stained-glass window, and he wandered over in hopes he might find the church unlocked.

He felt a heavy sigh of relief as the solid oak doors gave way easily under his weight. Once he was inside, the warm air enveloped him like a down comforter, and for just a fleeting second he thought about staying here until his shift ended. Who would know?

As he made his way inside, he felt a familiar sense of peace.

What was it about a church that produced serenity? he wondered, gazing out over the pews. It didn't matter which one he stepped into, they all made him feel the same.

Toward the right of the altar, a single candle burned underneath the statue of Saint Anthony, and Hill found himself following its light like a lost ship sailing toward a lighthouse.

By the time he had reached the front of the church, feeling had returned to his limbs. He peeled off his gloves and stood staring up at the life-size statue.

It was the most beautiful statue he had ever seen. The finely chiseled stone appeared almost lifelike, especially around the eyes, which carried a deep, soulful look of compassion. Without conscious thought, he reached out and touched the friar's robes, a part of him half expecting to feel the soft folds of fabric beneath his fingers, and he was faintly surprised when he connected with the cold, hard touch of unyielding stone.

As a member of the Salvation Army, Hill knew little about Catholic saints, but suddenly he found himself mesmerized by this strangely compelling statue. Saint Anthony was slightly bent over the infant Jesus, whom he held in his arms. His eyes were filled with adoration; his lips curved in a gentle smile. Most intriguing was the way the artist had captured the special bond between the saint and the child. The love they shared was almost palpable.

He gazed quietly up into the saint's gentle face, wondering why this simple form had seemed to touch him so deeply.

A prayer card was lying at the saint's feet. He picked it up and began to read.

O holy Saint Anthony, gentlest of saints, your love for God and charity for his creatures made you worthy, when on earth, to possess miraculous powers. Miracles

*waited on your word, which you were ever ready to
speak for those in trouble or anxiety. Encouraged by this
thought, I implore you to obtain for me my request.*

*The answer to my prayer may require a miracle; even
so, you are the saint of miracles.*

*O gentle and loving Saint Anthony, whose heart was
ever full of human sympathy, whisper my petition into
the ears of the sweet infant Jesus, who loved to be folded
in your arms, and the gratitude of my heart will ever be
yours.*

Maybe it was the hushed quiet in the sanctuary, or the
strange connection that he suddenly felt to this saint, but something propelled him to reach for a taper and light a candle of
his own. A small yellow flame slowly danced to life, bringing
with it a warm sense of peace.

Hill lived in a small furnished apartment on top of John
Moran's real estate office, on Main Street, six doors down from
Town Hall. It consisted of three small rooms. The kitchen was
the size of a broom closet but good enough for a bachelor who
ate most of his meals at the Country Kettle. He hadn't used
the living room since moving here, mostly because the couch, a
castoff from John's lake house, smelled of mold. A small bathroom was wedged in between the living room and kitchen, tiled
in institutional pea green, with a claw-foot tub.

Hill spent most of his time in the tiny bedroom that fronted
Main Street, watching the twenty-four-inch Samsung color
television that sat on top of his dresser; or, when weather permitted, leaning out the front window and waving to folks as
they passed by. Hill felt it gave citizens a sense of comfort,

knowing that a member of the Dorsetville Police Department was keeping a keen eye on things around town.

Tonight he entered the apartment numb from the cold and longing for a hot bath and a cup of tea. The thermostat was in the kitchen, and he pumped it up to the max before turning the jet on underneath the teapot. Not bothering to take off his coat, he foraged for a tea bag in the cabinet above the sink and plopped it into a recently acquired Starbucks mug before heading toward his bedroom.

The television remote was sitting by the side of his bed. He clicked it on, dropped it onto his bed, then started to shed his clothes.

"Are you tired of the direction your life has taken?" a man's voice queried. *"Tired of living from paycheck to paycheck? Tired of missing out on those promotions? Tired of watching others succeed while you remain stuck in the same drudgery, day in and day out? Do you long to turn your dreams into reality?"*

Hill turned to study the man's face framed in the television. Dark chestnut hair expensively cut, threaded with just enough gray to elicit the trust that came with age; square face, strong jaw, and steely blue eyes that pulsated with vitality. This was the image of a man who was the master of his fate, the captain of his soul.

"My name is Rich Malone and I'm about to introduce you to something that will radically change your life forever."

Hill loosened his top shirt button and sat down on the edge of his bed.

"I was once sitting right there where you are right now."

Hill glanced around his microscopic bedroom.

"That's right. I had lost my self-esteem. Life was hardly worth living. I could barely pull myself up out of bed every

morning. I was stuck in a dead-end job making minimum wage. I had few friends, and when I looked down over the years, I couldn't see any prospect of it ever changing. So, what turned my life around?"

Hill edged a little closer to the television set. Yeah, how did he do it?

"One day, I happened to stumble across the most incredible discovery. I discovered that a man's thoughts had the power to direct his life. That's right. 'As a man thinketh, so is he,' says the Bible.

"In other words, think great thoughts and you'll do great deeds. Think self-defeating, 'I can't ever win' thoughts, and that's what will materialize in your life.

"So I started a training program. I began to recondition my mind to accept only success, and the most exciting thing happened. Opportunities started coming my way, and within the span of one year's time, I went from working for someone else for minimum wage to owning my own company. That was ten years ago. Now I travel around the world, I own my own yacht, a private jet, three gorgeous homes, and best of all, I'm married to a wonderful wife and we have two great kids."

The camera panned a dazzling white beach on a backdrop of cerulean blue water; a Bentley with a mirrorlike finish, parked in front of a palatial home; then on to a portrait of Rich, his curvaceous wife, and two golden-haired children, gathered around a living room that looked as though it had been lifted from *Architectural Digest*.

Hill compared his own bleak existence. He looked out his apartment window, which fronted Stone's Hardware Store, thought about his secondhand pickup truck and the fact he hadn't had a date in nearly four years, and wondered if Rich's program could transform his life.

"*And I'm not just talking about material goods,*" Rich continued. "*This power can also help restore relationships that you might have thought never could be repaired.*"

Hill's thoughts shifted onto Sheriff Bromley as the camera came back to Rich seated on an expensive inlaid desk, his legs casually crossed, revealing a pair of handmade Italian loafers.

"*Now, the lifestyle that I've just described can be yours. How? By carefully following my twelve-step program, which I call Tapping the Power Within.*"

Beside Rich was a carefully displayed assortment of workbooks and several audiocassettes. Rich held one up to the camera.

"*The secret to my success lies right here, folks. It's a life-changing program designed to take you from living an ordinary, humdrum life to experiencing what thousands of those who have already used this program have discovered—whatever you can conceive, you can achieve.*"

Hill repeated the phrase. It rolled off his tongue like liquid gold. Maybe this was just what he needed to turn his life around.

"*This program is designed to help you tap into the limitless supply of power that resides within each of us, and all of this can be yours for the incredibly low price of just three hundred and fifty dollars, payable in three easy installments. Just call us at the number now flashing across your screen, and begin your own success story. Become a giant among men.*"

"A giant among men." He liked that.

"*Now let's hear some testimonies of those who have used my program to go from losers to winners.*"

While the camera flashed onto a young, healthy, athletic-looking couple frolicking outside a seaside resort, Hill started dialing.

Chapter Two

Doc Jack Hammon hadn't needed an alarm clock since his college days. He woke every morning at five, clear-eyed and ready to begin a day that usually didn't end until ten or eleven at night. Such were the ways of a country doctor.

But this morning he felt a little sluggish, as though his internal engine weren't firing on all pistons. It happened a lot lately. He chalked it up to age and a heavy workload. Doc Hammon's patient base was growing older, requiring more care.

He slipped out of bed in the predawn darkness to the rhythm of his wife, Joan's, gentle snores and fumbled for his robe, which had slipped off the bottom of the bed. A sharp breeze sliced in through the partially opened window. He paused to take in a deep breath, savoring the sweet smell of pine trees and apple-wood chimney smoke.

He gently closed the bedroom door and headed toward the kitchen. His bedroom slippers made a soft squishing sound along the wooden floors that Joan kept polished to a meticulous satin sheen. Looney Tunes, the cat whom the grandkids had named but whose name had since been reduced to just Tunes, heard his approach and thumped noisily to the floor, knowing that food was on the way.

Doc often joked that the cat had won the cat lotto. The gray-and-white, seriously overweight feline had just appeared one day at their back door and decided to stay. Since then, he whiled away the days atop the kitchen table, which Joan had placed beneath the back window. It provided a clear view of the woods and the swamplands. Further entertainment was produced by a row of bird feeders strung on the lower branches of the maple tree that shaded the patio in the summer.

Doc studied the feeders now. As the first shards of morning light filtered in through the trees, a bevy of scrabbling birds—blue jays, chickadees, and crows—flew in, stoic winged creatures who braved the harsh New England winters by depending on the good nature of bird lovers like his wife. They gathered now in a mad frenzy, each vying for a place around the feeders. The blue jays, an aggressive breed, got the first pick.

This morning, Tunes seemed indifferent to the activity outside. Instead, he grew impatient for his breakfast and began to meow loudly, rubbing up against Doc's legs.

"I'm coming," he told the cat, bending down to rub him between his ears. But Tunes slipped away, scurrying over to the cabinet where the cat food was stored as though to say, "In case you've forgotten, she keeps it in here. Now hurry!"

Doc left Tunes crunching this week's sampling of feline cuisine (Joan changed brands every other week—"He gets bored," she insisted) and went to shave and shower. Forty minutes later, both he and the cat stepped out the front door.

A ridge of pencil-thin light cowered behind a billow of clouds as Doc stepped through the front gate. He had gone only a few feet when a bitter chill snaked its way down the back of his neck. He raised his collar and wondered if spring would ever come.

Just last week, icicles had shattered against the sidewalks, and the town's crew had begun their great sweep, clearing months of sand and rock salt from the roads. Hopes had run high for a final end to winter, which had held the small valley hostage for months.

For a marvelous few days, spring had sung an adagio filled with the soft tremors of birdsong; and the lyrical flow of running brooks had combined in syncopation with the soft sway of treetops lulled by a gentle breeze.

This delightful prelude had sent Reverend Curtis, president of the Dorsetville Garden Club, and most of his members into action, ready to implement their annual spring cleanup drive. The poor Garden Club. He imagined them now, returned to their cozy kitchen tables to leaf through seed catalogs and to indulge in dreams of spring with heavy disappointment.

Soon the outline of his house faded in the distance. He always felt a certain melancholy in leaving it behind. As fanciful as it might seem, the house was more than wood and stone to him; it seemed somehow alive.

It had been his home since boyhood; he had inherited it from his father. He knew every nook and cranny, all its idiosyncrasies—if you banged on the wall left of the fireplace, the pipes would stop rattling upstairs; if the hall radiator began to hiss, a half turn to the valve would settle it right down.

It was a sprawling, two-story white colonial set on four acres of land within walking distance of the center of town. His father's old office was annexed on the west side, and Joan had turned it into a sunroom. They had raised their three children here and now enjoyed their grandchild's footsteps resounding along the same wood floors. He welcomed the sound. The house seemed so large for just two people, and Lord knows, it certainly was a dog to heat. But he couldn't imagine living anywhere else, and fortunately, neither could Joan.

He felt his pace quicken. He loved walking and had never considered it exercise. It was more a balm for his soul, a time of solitude and reflection. He especially liked his early morning walks. Sometimes it felt as though he were the only one in the world, treading new pathways unsullied by other travelers. Walking allowed him to gather his thoughts, plan his day, and on many occasions, pray uninterrupted. As he had once told Father James, some of his most earnest prayers had been said beneath the open skies.

So regardless of the weather, folks in town knew that every morning right after dawn and sometimes late at night (if he was concerned over a difficult case), Doc could be found walking along Main Street. Wonderful memories were stored along this half mile of asphalt. He never tired of trotting its course.

Dorsetville had been a great place to grow up in, and as far as he was concerned, it still was. He remembered his youth fondly. Days seemed a constant stream of motion; there were acres of forest to explore, the river, biking down country lanes, and of course, pushing scooters along Main Street.

The sight of the old marquee outside the Palace Theater always brought a flood of sweet memories. Saturday matinees cost twenty-five cents and included three cartoons plus a feature film. Gene Autry was his all-out favorite—*Back in the Sad-*

dle, *Bells of Capistrano, Rim of the Canyon*. He would sit on the edge of his chair, his eyes glued to the wide screen, cheering his hero on as he went about saving the West from yet another round of bandits.

A far less happy memory was the movie *Old Yeller*. It was the first time a movie had ever made him cry, and he had distrusted Walt Disney ever since.

The incline grew steeper. He bent into the hill, feeling his legs tighten, his chest constrict. Halfway up the incline, he grew winded. He really did have to lose some weight. But within five minutes, the ground leveled off and he turned left onto Main Street, beginning the loop that would take him around the business district, then up to Saint Cecilia's in time for morning mass.

Afterward, he would grab another cup of coffee at the Country Kettle and one of Lori Peterson's cinnamon buns still warm from the oven before trekking back home to pick up his car. Then it was off to Mercy Hospital and rounds.

On the rare day when there were no patients to visit, he'd join his friends gathered around a wooden table at the restaurant and treat himself to a slab of ham and two eggs over easy, hang the cholesterol.

He noticed a light on toward the rear of the town's favorite eating place, signifying that Harry and Lori were fast at work, preparing the mountains of home fries and sweet confections that brought folks from miles around to sample their wares.

Much to the town's chagrin, their favorite eatery had been discovered by folks outside the valley. A restaurant reviewer from the *Hartford Courant* had given Harry's home fries a five-star rating. This autumn, for the first time in the restaurant's history, there were peopled lined outside along the sidewalk. The regulars had been reduced to ordering takeout and setting up folding chairs along the street. Fortunately, winter had come and the restaurant had been reclaimed by those who came for more than the home fries. They came to be with their friends.

Doc's eyes were drawn to a new window display in Stone's Hardware Store. He studied the high-powered leaf blower. It was one he had been meaning to buy. Maybe he should give Mark a call later and have him set one aside for him.

Next he studied the hunting gear. He was ten years old again, gazing lustfully at pup tents and fishing rods and the newest-model BB gun. As far as he and his friends were concerned, Stone's was better than any toy store.

But a boy didn't just casually walk inside and gaze around. One must have a purpose. These were hallowed halls, and entering their portals was like gaining entrée to some mystical inner sanctum. The dark, cavernous interior spoke of secret rites of passage filled with sacred implements used to fashion boys into men. The store even smelled special—a combination of aged wooden floors, sweat, and turpentine, all tinged with the acrid scent of metal tools and copper pipes.

It was the favorite hangout of Doc's father, Jack senior.

He loved every square inch of it and seldom left without making a purchase that was cause for great alarm to Doc's mother. Once his father had a new tool, he felt duty-bound to use it. Unfortunately, his father was the world's worst handyman, and these attempts were always laced with trouble. His father would march with confidence, new tool in hand, in the direction of the needed repair, but invariably there would follow swearing and the calling upon the mercy of God, followed swiftly by a panicked scream for someone to get a tradesperson.

These calls were always placed by his mom and began with

"Come quick," followed by a short descriptive phrase . . . "He tried to fix the drain on the tub and now there's water pouring down through the ceiling."

He may have been a poor repairman; no one, however, could ever match his father's doctoring skills. He was one of those rare physicians who knew the wisdom in treating his patients as a triad—body, mind, and spirit. Doc could remember many a late-night knock on the back door when he was a young boy, a voice edged in torment, and a figure being led to his father's study for a glass of whiskey and a kind ear. His father often said, "Disease rests mostly in a man's soul. Those who are at peace with themselves and their maker are seldom ill." It was a recipe that Doc had also found to be true.

Doc would never forget the day that he had followed his father inside the hardware store to remind him of his upcoming birthday. There was a particular pocketknife that he had been coveting for weeks.

Suddenly Joe Platt came charging in through the back door, his face as white as pastry flour, screaming that old Mr. Stone was bleeding to death. The family patriarch had tried to fix Joe's hay bailer and had gotten his arm caught in one of the combines. Jack senior raced outside, with young Jack and his friends nipping at his heels—a severed limb was nothing to miss.

The boy stood riveted, watching blood pooling around Mr. Stone's severed arm. Could any man lose that much blood and live? he wondered. But his father seemed undaunted.

"You're going to be fine," he told Mr. Stone with a strength of conviction that immediately set the old man at rest.

Then he issued three sharp, rapid-fire orders that sent men scurrying.

"Al, call the ambulance. Dan, fetch that bottle of whiskey that's under the register. Fred, give me your belt. Jackson, you help Fred hold him down while I apply the tourniquet."

While young Jack's friends zeroed in on the lifeless arm wedged into one of the combines (destined to become the epicenter of conversations for the next several years), Jack focused on his father, the surety of his hands as he stemmed the bleeding, the look of trust that passed between old Mr. Stone and his dad. The boy's career choice was solidified that day.

The Open sign switched on at the Country Kettle. Doc pushed back his coat sleeve and looked at his watch. Mass started in twenty minutes. Plenty of time for a quick cup of coffee.

He waded across the main thoroughfare, which was thick with slush and glazed over with ice. It crackled under the soles of his rubber gum shoes. He was thinking about having a buttered roll with his coffee when he felt a pressure just below his collarbone. It felt as though a tourniquet were being drawn up around his chest. His breathing became labored and perspiration covered his face.

Suddenly all the symptoms he had been experiencing came together—shortness of breath, a sense of tiredness, a dull ache along his upper left arm. Doc had been a physician far too long not to recognize the first warning signs of a heart attack; still, the realization that he was not immune to this particular ailment caught him somewhat by surprise.

He slowed his pace, testing to feel if the pressure was growing more intense. Fortunately it was abating; still he knew that this was something that must be addressed immediately.

As the warm glow of lights spilling out from the Country Kettle's picture window beckoned, he slowly made his way toward his office to place a call to his cardiologist.

The morning was as crisp as a new dollar bill as the Gallagher twins labored up the steep incline, their breath rising on the cold March air like the steam of a locomotive. The school boiler was out, giving the children of Dorsetville an unexpected holiday.

The kitchen phone rang right after Tom Chute from the local radio station announced that the elementary school was closed for the day. It was Bobbie Moran asking if Dexter's hockey team, the Headbangers, was up for a match against the Icebreakers.

"Sure, if you promise not to go home crying like a bunch of babies when we beat the pants off you," Dexter swaggered.

Bobbie countered by calling Dexter's team a bunch of faggots, reminding Dexter they held a two-game lead, and saying that the Headbangers couldn't beat an egg yolk, let alone his team. The boys hurled a few extra insults before finally agreeing to meet at Fenn's Pond in two hours.

Dexter was desperate to win this match. He hated being on the losing end of anything. In fact, he was so determined to take every advantage he could, he even snuck inside his parents' room and said a prayer in front of a small statue of Saint Anthony that his mother kept on her bedroom dresser. The Headbangers had gotten stuck with the Martin brothers this season, a decided handicap. Everyone knew that the Martins played like sissies. Dexter figured he could use every advantage he could get.

Skates were flung across their backs, metal runners glistening in the bright sun, as the twins labored up the sharp slope leading to the pond. Also weighing Dexter down was the plastic bag filled with three dozen chocolate chip cookies that his mother had baked this morning for her quilting group. They were guaranteed to give him a case of hives that would make him itch like a dog with fleas, but Dexter didn't care. He was saving them for after the game—his victory fare. He'd worry about rashes later.

The swish of skates crisscrossing the ice sounded as the brothers neared the rise. Dexter's heart sank. Drats! He'd wanted to get here first, have the ice to themselves so they could practice some new moves. Just like Bobbie Moran to beat him to it. He was such a dirtbag.

"Here come the losers," Bobbie taunted, making a smart turn and coming to an abrupt stop.

"You got here early," Dexter said, trying not to let his disappointment show.

"We thought we'd get in a little extra practice."

"You must really suck, if you need *that* much practice," he taunted, dropping his skates on the ground.

"What? You afraid that we're going to beat you geeks?" Brad Stone asked, joining in.

"Who are you calling a geek?" Dexter challenged, rising to the insult.

Rodney grabbed his arm. "Let it go, man. It's not worth getting into a fight over. We'll lick them on the ice."

"Yeah, yeah." Dexter shrugged his arm free.

The twins watched their opponents hit off some practice shots. They missed four out of ten. Dexter's mood lightened. Maybe things weren't so bad after all.

Over the next twenty minutes, the rest of the team members arrived, along with Linda Kilbourne and her twin sister, Leah, their self-appointed referee.

"Hi, guys," Leah said, pulling a whistle out from her parka.

No one would acknowledge her. Instead the boys pretended disinterest, although every one of them had a secret crush on this flaxen-haired tomboy. Leah would have been appalled at these secret thoughts.

She could care less about geeky things like boys. This budding beauty came for one reason only. She loved sports. Any kind of sport—hockey, softball, soccer, tennis, football. She played all with equal confidence. If only she could be out there today, feel the sharp wind sting her face, the stretch of her body as she maneuvered into position, pulling back hard on the stick and letting the puck sail right past the goalie and into the net.

Leah watched the boys fumbling around, as clumsy as a bunch of puppies, and knew she could lick any one of them; but a lengthy eye operation this past fall had benched her for the season. She had had to settle for refereeing.

"Hello," Linda called sweetly to Dexter. Unlike her sister, Linda was very much into boys, particularly Dexter.

The object of her affection kept his face down, refusing to respond.

"You could at least say hello," she teased. "I came all the way out here in the cold just to see you play."

The other boys had picked up on the conversation. They clustered into a group and began to snigger.

Dexter's face had turned three shades of red. "Linda Kilbourne, you're a stupid pig. Why don't you go home?" he shouted.

"Stop pestering Dexter," Leah told her sister, elbowing her in the ribs.

"Ouch!"

"He's here to play hockey, not to make goo-goo eyes at you." Linda was such a ninny. It was hard to believe they were twins.

Linda laughed. "I'm not pestering him. I'm here to cheer for his team."

"I'm here to cheer for his team," Dexter's teammates mimicked, doubling over with laughter.

Dexter wanted to kill her. Yuck! What did it take to get rid of her, anyway? He had tried just about everything—inked the handle to her locker, hailed down insults, pelted her with water balloons, snatched her book bag and hoisted it up into a tree; but she kept coming back. She was a regular Energizer Bunny.

But he was cooking up a scheme that should end her pestering him once and for all. It involved locking her in old man Thompson's outhouse and pushing it down the small cliff next to his house, which would probably land him in more trouble than the time he and Rodney had accidentally blown up Mr. Hornibrook's boat, but he figured it was worth it.

"Hey, guys," Brad Stone yelled from the far side of the pond. "The ice over here is starting to break up. We'd better move the boundaries."

"Everybody got that?" Leah asked, skating onto the ice.

She ordered the teams into position. The boys obeyed without comment.

"Four twenty-minute periods," Leah instructed. "A two-minute penalty for all body checking, holding, slashing, and tripping guys with your sticks," she announced. "Any questions?"

"Yeah, what are these sissies going to do when they lose?" Bobbie teased.

"Who are you calling a sissy?" Dexter sneered.

Leah dropped the puck. All insults immediately stopped.

Lorraine Gallagher looked at the empty cookie sheets and shook her head. Those little rascals. What was she going to do with them? If she weren't still dressed in her nightgown and robe, she'd get the car out and snatch them back home.

Oh well. It was too late now anyway. The twins had probably finished the batch and would be a mess of hives within the hour. She sighed in exasperation, then went to the freezer and pulled out a Sara Lee French cheesecake to replace the cookies. Fortunately, there was still plenty of time for it to defrost before her quilting group arrived.

Which reminded her, she had better get going. The boys had made a mess of the upstairs bathroom. It would have to be scrubbed out. The living room needed to be vacuumed; Rodney had spilled a jar of peanuts all over the carpet. And the breakfast dishes were still in the sink. She'd tackle them first. Rolling up her sleeves, she ran some hot water, squirted in some detergent, then waited for the water to cover the tops of the dishes. Plunging her hands into its warm depths, she let her mind drift as she mechanically scrubbed and scoured.

A large window sat above the sink, overlooking an apple orchard. How barren the landscape appeared this time of year, she mused while rinsing off two glasses and setting them on the drain board. She would be so happy when spring finally arrived. She had grown tired of a landscape colored in browns and grays.

House sounds filled the quiet morning air. The burner kicked on downstairs. Seconds later, the sound of hot water gurgled as it filled the cast iron radiators. A floorboard creaked. A window frame rattled in the wind. All familiar, comforting sounds.

She hadn't always considered them such. At first she had found them alarming, certain that something had to be wrong, especially with the plumbing. Radiators had never sounded like that while she was growing up in an apartment in downtown Hartford. But in time she learned to love the sounds because she loved the house.

She remembered the first time she and Mike had seen their home. They had been heading up north en route to her aunt Myrtle's home in Barrington, Vermont, when Mike had taken a wrong turn.

"Where are we?" she asked.

"The sign says Dorsetville," Mike answered, slowing down to let a truck pass.

The closer they drew to the center of town, the more their excitement grew. There was no denying that the town appeared tattered and in need of a complete overhaul, but hidden underneath layers of peeling paint and sagging porches were architectural details that spoke of a once-prosperous era.

Elaborate trim work surrounded doors and windows; classic Greek columns flanked the Town Hall, along with an intricately carved cherub poised above the doors. Farther along the main thoroughfare, old Victorian homes flanked wide avenues, adorned with gingerbread porches and leaded-glass windows. They, too, looked as though they needed a little TLC, but nothing could detract from their classic design.

"We have a few extra minutes. Let's take a tour around the area before turning back," she said enthusiastically.

"Sounds good to me," Mike agreed.

Although neither voiced a hope that this might be the place they had been searching for (a quaint New England town where they could afford to purchase a home and raise a family), each felt the first faint stirrings of excitement.

Up until now, their search had been met with disappointment. Their budget was tight, which meant anything they looked at had to be fixer-upper. Their dream was to find a period home that they could take from ramshackle to showplace. Both were extremely handy and therefore confident that they could pull it off. Mike knew a fair amount about carpentry, and she was an accomplished seamstress. But much to their chagrin, they found that most older homes in need of restoration had already been snatched up by savvy New Yorkers as weekend getaways. Still, they continued to dream.

Then Mike rounded a bend and they saw a For Sale sign at the end of a long dirt driveway.

"What do you think?" Mike asked, leaning over the steering wheel. "Should we take a look?"

"Absolutely!" she shouted.

Trees and bushes overgrown from years of neglect snatched at the car's fenders as Mike slowly navigated through the thick woodland. The driveway suddenly took a sharp left and to their utter delight revealed the outline of an old Greek Revival home that stood empty.

They hopped out of the car and bounded about like children at Christmas, and even though the house was badly in need of paint, the back porch rotted through, the yard overgrown with enough weeds to choke a goat, and several of the shutters were lying at odd angles, it was love at first sight. They decided, however, to wait for the realtor before exploring the inside.

The For Sale sign told them to contact realtor John Moran, which they did immediately and made plans to view the inside of the home the following Saturday. Never had seven days seemed so interminable, but the wait proved worth it.

As soon as John opened the front door and they stepped through, they knew they had found their home. A charming entry hall ran the length of the house. The front portion was bedecked by a graceful curved staircase that elegantly looped around the entire space like a lady's silk wrap. The couple pounded up the stairs, opening and closing doors. There were three small bedrooms and a tiny bathroom that at one time seemed to have been a closet. Dreams and talk of renovations—they would move this wall, place a window seat along here, wallpaper one section, paint another—took seed at that moment.

Downstairs to the right of the staircase was a large living room with nine-foot ceilings and a hand-carved fireplace surround that created a natural focal point. A small front parlor that led to the dining room sat to the left of the staircase, which had two built-in corner cupboards.

A rather large but antiquated kitchen stood at the rear of the house, with a side door that connected to a small storage shed. Lorraine let Mike wander through that section alone while she watched from the safety of the kitchen.

"Hey . . . there's a nest of mice in here," he called out, delighted as any schoolchild.

As unsettling as the thought of mice scurrying past her might have been, it didn't stop Lorraine from encouraging Mike to make an offer, and to their delight, it was accepted. They had a double celebration that evening. Lorraine had also discovered that she was pregnant with twins.

Within two months, while Mike commuted an hour and a half to and from work, she painted and sanded their new home, and fashioned bolts of fabric into curtains and spreads, while trying not to be alarmed when she heard something scratch behind the walls, or a floorboard creak upstairs in the attic, or the radiators hiss. The women who came from all parts of town to welcome her to Dorsetville tried to allay her fears.

"Oh, you'll get used to it in time," Harriet Bedford assured her, unloading a trunkful of perennials as part of the Dorsetville Garden Club's welcome gift.

Ethel Johnson showed up next with a casserole and the name of a local plumber. "Harriet said you needed your radiators bled. Just give Pete a call. He'll come right out."

Marge Peale arrived a few weeks later. She and the judge had been off on a cruise, she said, or she would have been here earlier. And when she learned that Lorraine often felt anxious all alone in the country, she offered a solution.

"You need to learn to quilt. It will take your mind off things."

But Lorraine had seen the beautifully crafted quilts hung on clotheslines around town. "I could never make one of those," she said.

"Nonsense. If you can sew a straight line, you can quilt," Marge insisted, and she was right.

That was ten years ago, and since that time Lorraine had sewn dozens of beautiful quilts. Last year her Rose of Sharon, a pink-and-green appliqué on a white background with a large hand-quilted medallion in the center, had won honorable mention at the Goshen Fair.

A dark cloud slid across the sun, pitching the kitchen into darkness. She reached for a towel, dried her hands, and threw on the overhead light. She sure hoped it wasn't going to snow again. She was tired of snow. She looked at the kitchen clock. Oh dear, she had petered away most of the morning. She had better hustle. The boys would be back soon for lunch and the quilters were coming at one o'clock.

The hockey game was nearing its finish. The boys' faces were bright red from both the bitter cold and the exertion. There was a lot riding on this game as the sun tucked itself behind a bank of clouds.

Both teams had played hard, holding nothing back. During the first period, the Headbangers were leading seven to four, but then Rodney hit the puck out of the pond. That lost their team two points.

Second period, the Icebreakers scored three goals in a row, each one sailing past the Martin brothers; and then Leah had issued an offside call to the Headbangers, which no amount of arguing or intimidating tactics could make her rescind.

"You crossed their line before the puck." She held out stubbornly.

Of course, the Icebreakers insisted she was right. Dexter's team insisted just as hard that she was wrong. She was a girl. What did she know? Dexter resumed his position only at the threat of another penalty, which intensified his general hatred of all girls.

They were down to the last five minutes of the game. The Headbangers had managed to pick up several extra points, mostly because Brad Stone had been benched for tripping the Martin brothers with his stick.

The Headbangers were leading. Then, in quick succession, the Icebreakers scored two points. Freddie Luttman, the Headbangers' goalie, took a puck to the helmet but saved the Icebreakers from scoring the next point. The force of the blow, however, had caused his teeth to go right through his tongue. Blood spurted everywhere. Leah gave the time-out sign and skated over.

"I think you'd better go see Doc Hammon," she said sagely.

Freddie refused. A wound received in defense of the team gave a guy a certain social standing. He meant to stick around and milk it for all it was worth.

"Whoa . . . that's a lot of blood," Chuck Martin said, fascinated by the bright red stain spreading across Freddie's nylon ski parka.

"Aaaa . . . it's nothing," Freddie said proudly. Later, the injury would cost him two stitches and a tetanus shot that hurt like the dickens, but for now he was enjoying the glory.

Finally there were two minutes left to the game. The score was tied. The captains called a time-out and huddled with teammates to plan their next move.

"We make the next goal, and we win the game," Dexter said, as though he were telling his teammates something they didn't know. "Now here's my idea."

The circle tightened.

"Rodney . . . when the puck crosses over the center line, skate in front of Bobbie and stay there. You got it?"

"I've got it."

"Martins, you keep the right sidelines clear. And don't mess it up."

"We won't. Promise."

"And what will you be doing?" Rodney asked.

"Never mind. You just do what I told you and I'll take care of the rest."

The whistle blew. Leah stood ready to resume the game.

Dexter skated over to center field.

"Ready?" Leah asked.

"Ready," the team captains yelled in unison.

"Play," she shouted, then quickly backed away.

Bobbie captured the puck with lightning speed and passed it off to a teammate, who in turn skated furiously off toward the net, but Rodney was there to meet him.

The boy made a tight circle and passed it back to Bobbie. But there was no time for Bobbie to maneuver his body and line up the shot, so he was forced to swing around in a tight arch. Dexter had snuck up behind him and deftly stole the puck.

He kicked off with an inordinate amount of power and sailed across the ice. This time, true to their word, the Martin brothers swooped in and successfully ran interference. Dexter could almost taste victory.

He felt as though he were flying—the scenery lost in a giant blur—keeping the puck close to his skates, weaving the stick back and forth in tight, controlled movements. He blocked out everything else except that puck, driven by one thought and one thought only. He needed to reach the spot just short of the melting ice. From this vantage point he'd have a clean shot right into the net.

Brad Stone had been allowed back into the game and was right on Dexter's tail. Dexter bent low to the ice, tail up, shoulders down like a souped-up racing car. His legs pumped like pistons. He could feel Brad's hot breath against the back of his neck. You're almost there, he told himself. His teammates were in position. He had a clear shot to the net. A few seconds more.

Dexter caught Brad's shadow out of his left eye. His opponent had gained several critical feet. Drats! There was no way he could execute the shot with Brad positioned there. Dexter thought quickly, spun around, and headed in the opposite direction. The move caught Brad off guard. There was no time for him to recover. He had given Dexter the opening he needed.

From some distant place, Dexter heard his teammates shouting, "Dexter! Turn back! The ice is too thin over there!"

He tried to turn but it was too late. His foot seemed to give out underneath him as the ice began to crack. Within seconds, he went down.

The feeling came out of nowhere. One moment, Lorraine was scrubbing the upstairs bathroom sink, and the next she could hardly breathe. A strange tightness had settled just below her rib cage, followed by a chilling sense of unrest. She stood up, looked at her face in the bathroom mirror, puzzled. Where was this coming from? She had nothing to be anxious about.

Suddenly, she knew. Her sons were in dire trouble. She raced down the staircase, nearly tripped over the hem of her robe, and barreled out the front door.

"Dexter!" Rodney screamed, watching his brother disappear below the icy water. He kicked off and headed in the direction of the gaping black hole.

"Rodney, don't!" Leah shouted. "You'll fall through, too."

But Rodney heard nothing except the sound of his own racing heart, and even though he was skating as fast as his feet could propel him across the ice, it seemed an eternity before he reached the other side of the pond.

"The ice is breaking up!" Bobbie screamed, his voice panic-stricken.

Just as Rodney began to look down, the ice broke away beneath his feet, plunging him down into the pond's frigid depths.

He took in a mouthful of water before kicking his feet hard and propelling himself up toward the surface. As soon as his head broke through the water, the children's screams began in earnest.

"Hold on, Rodney! We're coming!" Leah shouted. "Everyone lie down on the ice. Form a chain. Grab the person's feet in front of you. Bobbie, you're the strongest. Get out in front of the line. Use your hockey stick to pull Rodney out."

The two teams quickly went into action. Bobbie carefully edged as close to Rodney as he dared. He thrust the stick out.

"Grab it!"

Rodney tried to do as instructed, but there was something wrong. His mind kept telling his arms to move forward, grab hold of the stick, but they weren't moving. In fact, they felt as though they weighed a hundred pounds.

And he was cold, so cold. Icy water had seeped underneath his jacket. There was no feeling left in his feet, and he was suddenly overwhelmed with the urge to close his eyes and let the soft folds of sleep take him away.

"Come on, man. Stay with us, man. You can do it!" Bobbie screamed. "Reach for it."

The children began to yell in unison. *"Grab hold of the stick . . . Grab hold of the stick . . ."*

Leah didn't know what made her say it, but she found herself shouting, "Hurry up, Rodney. Pull yourself out so we can go and help Dexter."

Dexter . . . Yes, his brother needed his help. He dug deep down within himself, forcing his arms to move, and grabbed hold of the stick.

"Hang on, Rodney!" Bobbie shouted. "Everybody, pull!"

Sam Rosenberg was fit to be tied. He had bought a new Sears battery a year ago, which meant it still had four years left on its warranty. But this morning when he had gone out to start up his 1972 Plymouth Duster, all he got was *click . . . click . . . click*. The battery was dead.

He stomped back into his house and made a round of calls. Harriet would have to get a ride with Ethel this morning. Timothy and Ben were on their own, and Mrs. Hopkins over at the senior center was warned that she might have to find a substitute driver to deliver the Meals on Wheels.

Then he called Nancy Hawkins over at Tri Town Auto.

"Sorry, Sam, but it seems you're not the only one with a dead battery. Half the town has called wanting a jump start," she told him. "I'm afraid it's going to be a couple hours before I can get someone out to your place."

What could he do? So he waited.

Fortunately, Nancy showed up in time for him to still get the Campbells over to Doc Hammon's for Fred's appointment.

"I'll be there in fifteen minutes," he told Arlene. "Have Fred ready. Oh, and would you mind if afterward we took a trip over to Sears?"

Arlene lived just over the rise, about a mile and a half from the Gallaghers' place. Sam's mind was not on the road. It was on what he planned to tell the Sears salesclerk. He had just started to pass Fenn's Pond when something hit him as strange. Maybe it was the way the children were huddled together. He slowed to a stop and got out to investigate. Lorraine Gallagher was kneeling off to one side dressed only in a house robe. A child was cradled in her arms.

"Dear Father of Abraham," he whispered, and clambered up the hill.

"What happened?" he asked, watching Lorraine clutching Rodney's soaking wet body. Icicles clung to the boy's hair.

"Dexter fell through the ice," Leah said, her body shaking more from shock than from the cold. "Rodney tried to save him and then he fell through, too."

Sam scanned the crowd. "Where's Dexter?"

Leah began to sob, unable to answer.

"He's still under the water," Bobbie Moran whispered, then turned away so no one could see his tears.

Chapter Three

*I*t was as though someone had blocked out the sun as a dark pall settled over the town. Suddenly everyday greetings such as "Do you think spring will ever come?" or "Have you started your seeds yet?" had been replaced with "Have you heard?"

Those who walked the streets that day seemed a little more hunched over, the weight of the tragedy bearing down heavily on each and every Dorsetville citizen. Parents and grandparents wept openly. Even Sheriff Bromley, a hardened professional, found his eyes misted over whenever someone asked, "Any news yet?"

Dorsetville folks thought of themselves as a family. Now, two of their children had slipped through the icy pond's surface. One was suffering from hypothermia and en route to

Mercy Hospital; the other still lay buried beneath the pond's frozen depths.

Betty Olsen, Dorsetville's police department dispatcher, had been reading an article on Oprah when Sam made the first call. It took her under a minute to track the sheriff down. He was having a cup of coffee with the town's fire chief, Bill Halstead. Bill immediately issued the alarm. Seconds later, the sounds of ice dripping off the roofs and winter sludge being shoveled off the sidewalks were drowned beneath the ear-piercing blast of sirens.

Timothy McGee had been seated inside Walt's Barbershop, getting a trim, when the siren blasted. The barbershop was directly across the street from the firehouse, providing a bird's-eye view as volunteers rushed to the station. Minutes later, the fire trucks and ambulance rolled out with horns blasting.

Mark Stone was lifting a thirty-pound bag of dog food into Ethel's car when they charged past.

"I wonder what's happened," he said to Ethel, who was trying to soothe Honey. Loud noises always made the dog nervous.

Shop owners and customers tumbled out onto the sidewalk. Speculation ran high. Could it be a fire? they asked, checking the sky for a sign of smoke. Or perhaps a car accident, which incited folks to ask, "Has anyone seen Deputy Hill?"

But news travels faster than the speed of light in the small town, and before the icing was dry on the petit fours that Lori Peterson had prepared for the Garden Club's monthly meeting, everyone knew that the Gallagher boys had had an accident and that Dexter was still trapped beneath the ice.

Throughout that morning, phones rang all over town with the devastating news of the twins' accident. All expressed their deep compassion for the parents. The grief they must be feeling was surely unbearable, many said. Most couldn't begin to imagine what it must be like to lose a child. But one person in town knew exactly the heart-wrenching sorrow the couple was experiencing, and her prayers went out to them.

Thirty years ago, Mrs. Norris had lost her own sweet Jennie beneath those inky waters. Her darling, blond-haired eight-year-old daughter had wandered out across the ice that warm winter day to rescue her new kitten. Both had drowned. It was an incident that folks around town carefully kept hidden, knowing the deep pain that was reflected in Mrs. Norris's eyes at its mention.

She had been folding wash on the kitchen table when Ethel called to tell her about the twins. The words, like hammer blows, brought her to her knees. Memories of that fateful day came flooding back. She struggled under their force. How could this have happened again? Another child lost to a watery grave. Her heart welled up with compassion for the parents, who she knew would spend the rest of their lives searching for something they might have done differently, desperately wishing to be given another chance.

Father James must be told immediately. She got to her feet, grabbing hold of a chair for support. He had driven to Southington to pick up the Lenten supplies at Patrick Baker's and hadn't planned to return until late afternoon. The Gallaghers would need his support, and the boy must be given the last rites.

"Oh . . . Father . . . ," she cried at the sound of his voice on the phone, incapable of saying more. The words had caught in her throat like a piece of poorly chewed meet.

Father James had never known Mrs. Norris to break down before and was instantly alarmed.

"What's happened?" he asked, a host of scenarios falling from the sky like hailstones, each more sinister than the previous one. Nothing, however, could have prepared him for her reply.

"It's the Gallagher twins," she choked out. "They've fallen through the ice over at the pond."

Under his coaxing, she was able to relay as many of the facts as she knew. School had been canceled, and the boys had gone over to the pond to play hockey.

"Rodney has been recovered and is en route to Mercy Hospital, but Dexter is still missing," she concluded, her mind momentarily shifting off the current tragedy and onto that fateful day thirty years ago.

Father James had been quietly listening without comment, but now, when he spoke, she could hear his own tears gathering.

"Does Mike know?"

"I don't think so, Father," she said, fighting to stay in the present.

"Call Al and tell him that I'll pick him up over at the plant."

Before he hung up, Father James asked her to cancel all his afternoon appointments. As she later scanned his date book, her eyes fell on the notation for four o'clock. Father James had penciled in, "Meet with altar servers for the Ash Wednesday service," and beneath that he had listed both Rodney's and Dexter's names.

Doc Hammon stood over Dexter's hospital bed and slipped a nitroglycerin tablet beneath the boy's tongue. Both his cardiologist and Joan would be livid if they knew he had stayed to work on the boy. No undue stress, he had been told, yet he had deliberately elected to disregard the order. He would not leave this child alone in the hands of others.

The room held an eerie silence, punctuated by the rhythmic hiss of the respirator as it forced air into an inert body. No trace of the child that had laughed and joked, filled with the zest of youth, now remained. That part of him had vanished beneath the pond's depths.

Miraculously the highly skilled medical staff had been able to reestablish a heartbeat, no small feat, since the boy's body temperature had plummeted dangerously low. It had taken them hours to bring it back to normal, increasing it no more than one degree an hour to avoid having the internal organs collapse under the stress.

For all of their efforts, the boy remained in critical condition. Dexter, who only yesterday had been so vibrant and full of life, now lay pale and lifeless against the white sheets, entangled within a network of wires and catheters and plastic tubing. In this state, he could survive indefinitely—weeks, months, perhaps even years. But no trick of science could revive the essence of the child, that special life-giving energy whose source will forever remain hidden, that which makes each of us unique. It was gone. The EEG monitor attested to that.

"Doctor?" a young nurse called, nervously pulling aside the curtain. She was a recent nursing school graduate and had been working here for less than a month. This was her first case involving a child, and it was evident by the emotions playing across her face that it had shaken her badly.

"The boy's parents keep asking. I don't know what to tell them."

"I'll be right out," he said, then seeing her distress, added gently, "Why don't you take a break? You look as though you could use a cup of coffee."

She nodded thankfully, quickly disappearing through the drawn curtain.

Doc watched the snow rapidly falling outside the window, blanketing the countryside in a cover of white down. He should have brought his heavier boots, he mused, lingering over the banal thought for several minutes, using it as an anchor to steady himself in this turbulent sea of grief.

But suddenly a wave of anger like a great tsunami surged from the depths of his soul, and with it an outpouring of fury.

Why, why, why had this happened? It was a stupid, senseless accident, preventable if only one adult had had the presence of mind to set up safeguards. Recent warm temperatures had undoubtedly softened the ice. Why hadn't anyone taken the time to check it out? Every parent knew that pond attracted kids like a magnet.

He took Dexter's small hand into his, a silent tear slipping down his cheek. His heart was heavy with grief because the medical profession he revered so highly had been unable to save this child. He took a deep breath, pushed the curtains aside, and headed out toward the waiting area, where he would confront the Gallaghers with the news that the essence of the son they loved was gone.

Mike and Lorraine were seated between Father James and Harriet. The wait had seemed interminable. Every time the door that linked the waiting room to the cubicles in the back opened, their hearts lurched, their breath stopped short, their eyes trained on the person emerging, hoping that someone was coming to give the news they craved. Dexter was going to be all right.

As the long wait stretched on throughout that day and late into the night, their fears fed on the silence, and they grew quiet, each locked in a private walled room of misery. Father James was especially concerned for Mike and Lorraine, who sat rigid, staring into space with a look of the weariness and horror one often saw on the faces of victims of war. Tears had stopped flowing hours ago. They had none left to give.

Harriet had long since grown weary of trying to find words of encouragement. She sat fingering her rosary while Father James studied the floor tiles.

Finally, the metal doors opened and Doc appeared. The quartet jumped to their feet, their faces anxious, their eyes trained like lasers on Doc's face.

"How are they?" Mike asked before he had taken a step. Lorraine reached for his hand.

"Let's start with the good news," Doc said, waving them back into their chairs. Mike remained standing.

"Rodney is doing well. He suffered a mild case of hypothermia, but his body temperature has been stabilized and he seems to be doing well. We don't know about the frostbite on his fingers or toes, but I don't believe it's severe enough to require amputations. We'll know for certain in a day or so. Meanwhile, I've given him something to help him sleep and for the moment he's resting comfortably. You can go visit him whenever you like."

"And Dexter?" Lorraine asked. The couple hadn't been allowed to see him.

Doc lowered his head, avoiding eye contact. "We were able to restore a heartbeat, but the EEG is flat."

"What does that mean?" Father James asked.

Doc fought to retain a professional distance that would allow him to deliver in clear, clinical, nonemotional tones the worst possible news any parent could ever hear, but it was difficult. This wasn't some faceless stranger. This was a child he had brought into the world. He had doctored him since he was an infant, had seen him through endless rounds of hives, multiple stitches, and several broken bones. Once he had even joined Father James in playing a practical joke on the boy in hopes of getting him and his brother to confess to having burnt down the Congregational church. And now . . .

In the end, he choked out the final diagnosis. "Your son is clinically dead. We did everything we could, but he was under the water too long to revive. I'm sorry."

The words cut through the room like a scythe. Mike dissolved into tears as Lorraine tumbled into his arms.

"You said that his heart is beating," Father James reiterated.

Doc nodded. "The respirator is feeding the heart oxygen right now, but when it's disconnected, the heart will stop and he will die."

"But for now, he lives," Father James reminded him. "And where there is life, there is hope. Let none of us ever forget that."

From somewhere in the distance, Rodney heard his mom and dad. They were crying. He tried to ask them what was wrong, but he couldn't get his mouth to work. It was as if his body and thoughts had somehow been disconnected. It should have frightened him, but it didn't. Instead, he felt a wonderful sense of peace and just let go. Oh well, he'd find out what was wrong later. For now, he just wanted to hang loose and enjoy this feeling of peace that enveloped him like a mother's caress.

Slowly, he began to feel himself being lifted. Higher and higher he went, like a kite. He should have been frightened, but he wasn't. In fact, it felt pretty cool. When he finally opened his eyes, he was amazed to discover that he was hovering over the town. He was flying!

He zoomed over Dorsetville, careening past Saint Cecilia's bell tower, then on to Main Street. Down below he watched as people he knew walked about. He spied Mr. Platt getting into his truck, and his teacher, Mrs. Clifford, going into the Country Kettle.

"Hi, Mrs. Clifford," he called, but she didn't seem to hear him.

Wow, wait until Dexter saw what he could do . . . Which reminded him—he hadn't seen his brother in a while. Where did he go?

The question seemed to draw him toward the pond, where both hockey teams congregated by the water's edge. He wondered why they weren't playing. A lot of adults were also there. He saw Sheriff Bromley and his dopey deputy. Leah Kilbourne and her sister were seated on a rock, and it seemed as though they were crying. Yuck! Girls!

"Hey! Look up here!" he shouted, but no one paid any attention to him. What was going on here? It wasn't much fun being able to fly if no one else could see or hear you.

Then he saw Dexter's hockey stick. It was lying there on the ice where anyone could come along and snatch it. That wasn't like Dexter.

"Hey, Dex," he called, hoping to spy him in the crowd below. "Where are you?"

"I'm over here," his brother answered.

The voice, however, didn't come from below, but from somewhere up above. Rodney searched around and spied a blinding ray of light beginning to circle around him.

"Dex?" he called, tentatively.

"Come on," Dexter said impatiently. "I can't wait much longer."

"But I can't see you."

"I'm over here."

"Where?"

"Listen, I gotta go. Tell Mrs. Norris that Jennie is here."

"Who's Jennie, and where are you going?"

"Tell her that she's all right and that she's come to show me the way."

"Dex, this isn't funny, man. Come on. Where are you?"

But Dexter didn't answer, and then the light disappeared.

Chapter Four

*B*y *the end of the week* there wasn't a person within a twenty-mile radius who hadn't heard about the Gallagher twins.

Small New England towns are always quick to respond to trouble with an outpouring of love and support, which in the Gallaghers' case was channeled through the countless casseroles and cakes that came rushing in like a flood. Two days after the accident, the Gallaghers' freezer was packed from top to bottom. By day three, the overflow made its way to Harry's walk-in freezer at the Country Kettle.

"Did you see the tray of roast chickens I put in here yesterday?" Harry asked his waitress, Wendy Davis, as he stood staring at a wall of frozen pies that hadn't been there the day before. "I put them right here up in front. Where'd they go?"

Wendy peered over his shoulder. "Harry, you couldn't find a full-size cow if it were standing straight up, with all that food packed in there."

"You're a big help. Don't you have an order coming up?" he said, stomping over to the blackboard to erase chicken pot pies from the day's list of specials.

"Could we have some more coffee?" Ben called.

"Next time around," she said, balancing plates of eggs sunny-side up, a stack of pancakes, an egg sandwich, and two cups of coffee.

When Wendy was first hired, folks took bets on whether or not she would make it across the room without an accident. So far, she'd never dropped a dish.

"The Henderson sisters dropped over a cake for the Gallaghers," she told Harriet, returning with the coffeepot. "They made me promise that I wouldn't freeze it, so it will have to be delivered right away. Something about the flowers might wilt."

"Oh dear," Ethel said with a sigh.

"I take it you're not too keen on her baking," Wendy said. Wendy was a woman who always got straight to the point.

"It's not her baking exactly . . ." Harriet hedged.

"The danged woman decorates her cakes with wildflowers," Timothy offered, holding his cup steady while Wendy filled it to the brim. He took his coffee black.

"And that is a problem because . . . ?"

"It has more to do with the bugs that hitch a ride on the flowers," Sam offered.

"So, what do you want me to do with the cake? Pitch it?"

"Heavens, no!" Ethel said, aghast.

The Hendersons' confections might provide a challenge to eat (Father James had swallowed a spider once), but their hearts were in the right place. If they discovered that their cake had been discarded they would be deeply hurt.

"So, let me get this straight. You *want* me to deliver a cake with bugs to the Gallaghers?"

"Well, no, dear," Harriet tried to explain. "Just check for any insects before you bring it over. That's what the rest of us do when they drop cakes off for one of the cake sales."

"Only in Dorsetville," Wendy said, shaking her head. "Sam, hand me that empty plate. So, how do I get in?"

"Key's under the mat," Ethel said.

"Doesn't anyone in this town worry about break-ins?"

"What for? No one in town owns anything worth stealing," Timothy parried.

"That would explain it," she said, clearing off the rest of the table in the blink of an eye.

"Anyone want more coffee?" she asked, balancing a stack of plates, two water glasses, and a Pyrex coffeepot. "And Harriet, if there's anything I can do . . ."

"Some of us are going over tomorrow to clean the house," Harriet said. "Rodney's being discharged in a day or two. We thought we'd get it ready."

"Count me in," she said.

"Hey, Wendy!" one of the town crew shouted, waving his hand in the air. "We need an order to go."

"What? Do I look like a taxi that you gotta wave me down?" she asked, heading over.

Sam reached for the sugar bowl. "Ben, you said you had some good news?"

"I wasn't sure if this was the right time to mention it," he hedged. "You know, with the Gallagher boys and all."

"We could all use some good news." Harriet felt she could sure use a lift after a steady week of trauma.

"In that case"—Ben's face brightened—"Carl Pipson asked Timothy and me to take charge of the programming while he's away on vacation."

Carl was the station manager at WKUZ, the local cable station where Ben and Timothy volunteered as cameramen.

"Congratulations," Sam said, patting his friends on their backs. "What does Carl want you to do while he's away?"

"Pretty much what we do every week. Tape the news for the *Around the Town* segment and make sure all the programs air on time. Things like that," Ben said. "That reminds me. I forgot to tell you, Tim, someone from the mayor's office called this morning and left a message. They said that Roger is going to issue a formal announcement this afternoon that he'll be running again in the fall, and wants us to air it on this week's segment."

"Isn't it kind of early in the year to make an announcement?" Sam asked. "It's only March."

"George Benson says he's going to run against him, so Roger wants to get a jump on things," Ben offered.

"George?" Sam couldn't think of a more unlikely candidate. "What does he know about running a town?"

"Nothing," Timothy volunteered. "He's just doing it to get a rise out of the mayor."

Deputy Hill trudged down the sidewalk, struggling against the wind, which had picked up enough force to heave a medium-size dog or a small child into the next county. He hunched forward against the gale and stoically continued his patrol along Main Street.

How he wished winter was over, but it seemed as though it might tramp right into April. He longed for spring—soft green buds, breezes tipped in hyacinths, the sound of birdsong. He had almost forgotten what it felt like to step outside without his nose hairs freezing.

Hill crossed from one side of Main Street to the other, thankful that this was his final loop around downtown. He had worked a midnight-to-eight shift and was bone tired. Not that he had expended a lot of energy. It was just plain boring, patrolling the same square mile hour after hour without interruption. At least during the day there were people to talk to and an occasional summons to issue.

He tried not to let things get him down, knowing that nightshift duty couldn't last much longer. According to Rich Malone and the first segment of *Tapping the Power Within,* "Thoughts are things," and since he had been thinking of nothing other than getting off night duty for weeks, he figured it was just a matter of time before he'd be back on days.

Hill had every confidence in this new self-improvement course and had wasted no time in implementing the program. As soon as it had arrived—twelve audiocassettes neatly arranged in a freestanding binder; Rich Malone's autobiography, *How I Went from Rages to Riches;* a plaque that read, "You are what you think about all day long"; and a personal organizer/calendar with an inspirational saying for each day of the week—Hill had hopped in his truck and driven straight to Kmart, where he bought a top-of-the-line portable cassette player for $49.95 and three packs of triple A batteries, plus a recharger.

The first lesson had been about setting concise goals.

"You can't get where you're going if you don't know where you're bound," Rich said, so Hill settled on three:

1. Get back on days
2. Drive the police cruiser again
3. Make sergeant

Currently he was working on *The Road to Riches Through*

Random Acts of Kindness. Such acts, Malone insisted, were the central point in ensuring personal success. Hill played the tape over and over again as he walked his lonely beat, the earphones hidden beneath the earflaps of his fur-lined hat.

Through some kind of cosmic law (which Hill was still having difficulty understanding even though he had listened to Malone's explanation a number of times), when a charitable act of kindness was performed, the universe made a deposit into your cosmic account, which could later be used to bankroll your journey to success. Malone also emphasized that these acts must always be done anonymously.

Hill immediately set out to search for an opportunity to invest in this cosmic banking system, but he was having trouble finding a need that hadn't already been answered.

Christian charity was like breathing to the folks in Dorsetville, so the pickings were slim. Helping the Gallagher family would have been his first choice, but from what he could see, that was pretty much taken care of. Someone was shoveling the driveway. Someone else was picking up their mail, and he knew the women in town had the housekeeping covered. Hill figured he'd have to be pretty diligent if he wanted to get first dibs at any charitable act in this town.

Just then the sheriff's Chevy Blazer made its way slowly down Main Street. Hill made a big show of checking the inspection sticker on a parked truck; then turned to shine a flashlight into the Japanese restaurant, as if checking on things inside. The sheriff turned down a side street just as the sun began to edge its way through a wall of clouds. Hill relaxed and adjusted his earphones.

He watched his reflection in the various storefront windows, noting new displays. As he neared Secondhand Rose, Beth and Bobbie Hamilton rapped from inside the window.

"What do you think?" Beth called, her voice muffled through the thick plate of glass.

Hill studied the mannequin. It was dressed in a loose-fitting flowery dress once owned by Marge Peale, with fake pearls brought in by the mayor's wife (the mayor had surprised her with a real pearl necklace for their twenty-fifth wedding anniversary), plus a matching wide-brimmed hat and sunglasses that Beth had tired of. It carried a basket filled with silk tulips and daffodils purchased on sale at Kmart.

Although Hill didn't know a thing about store displays, he gave it the thumbs-up, which seemed to please Beth and her sister immensely. They smiled with satisfaction.

Up ahead, the bell on the Country Kettle's front door jangled. A workman stepped out onto the sidewalk, carrying a takeout bag. The smell of rich coffee, crispy fried bacon, and buttery home fries wafted on a gentle breeze, reminding Hill that he hadn't had a morsel of food since coming on shift. That was eight hours ago. A plate of eggs over easy with slices of freshly baked bread would taste mighty good about now.

He checked his watch. He had another twenty minutes left to his shift and figured he could hold out that long. To keep his mind off his stomach grumblings, he checked alleyways and car stickers in hopes of speeding the time along.

With only a few minutes left to go, he headed back to the restaurant and noted that Sam's Plymouth was parked by the curb with a back window partially opened. The weatherman had predicted snow flurries later this morning. It would sure be a shame if Sam returned to find snow piled on the backseat.

As he expected, the car was unlocked, so he opened the door and rolled up the window. But just before he was about to slam it shut, he noticed the cable station's expensive video camera on the backseat.

"Holy Christmas!" he shouted. What was Sam thinking? Dorsetville might be about the safest place this side of heaven, but it was not immune to crime. Take Clyde Hessler, for instance. A few years back, he had sauntered into town and taken off with Barry Hornibrook's construction money, the money he had borrowed to turn the old mills into a hotel and conference center. So it followed that if one crook had found his way to their corner of the world, others might not be far behind.

Hill glanced through the restaurant windows. Sam and his friends were settled around their favorite table, their backs to the street. He shook his head. Anyone could have taken off with the camera without a soul noticing. There was only one thing to do. As deputy, Hill had an obligation to educate the town's citizens about crime prevention. He'd simply grab the camera, march into the restaurant, and give the men a stern lecture on safety.

He was about to reach for the camera, then suddenly stopped. Hadn't he been searching for an opportunity to perform a random act of kindness? Wouldn't preventing a robbery qualify?

He looked around the street. No one was watching. Diving into the backseat of the car, he closed the door and quickly scribbled a note, explaining the dangers of leaving an expensive piece of equipment in an unlocked car, and placed it where it was certain to be found. Then, checking to make certain that the street was still clear, he slipped out, locked the car, and resumed his patrol, smiling like a man who had found the secret of youth.

Although Father James seldom if ever took a nap, today he needed one badly. Kicking off his black loafers, he stretched full-out on the office sofa, tucked an arm behind his head, and tried to settle his thoughts enough to induce sleep. For some unfathomable reason, he was now suffering from insomnia. It had been days since he'd had a full night's sleep. The night he had sat vigil with the Gallaghers had turned his internal clock inside out.

The door to the small hallway that connected the church to the rectory slammed shut. The priest jerked into full consciousness. Mrs. Norris had returned from her scheduled hour of prayer. She was part of the round-the-clock prayer chain for Dexter.

He tried to settle back down, but found himself mentally tracing his housekeeper's footsteps. Water began to run into the sink. A cabinet door closed. A pan scraped against a metal burner on the stove. The refrigerator was opened and bowls were being pulled out and set on the nearby counter. She was making lunch.

He glanced at his watch. She always served lunch at twelve, which meant he had another thirty minutes to catch some shut-eye. He threw an arm over his face, blocking out a wedge of pale sunlight filtering in from the back window, and tried once again to quiet his thoughts. But like corks in a bottle, they continued to bob to the surface.

He still hadn't settled on a homily for the special mass the nuns at the Regina Francis Retirement Home had requested. It was to be said in honor of their founder, Sister Regina Francis. Tomorrow would have been her seventy-fifth birthday. Creating a homily for nuns was always a tricky business. They knew the catechism by heart. It came from years of teaching CCD classes. And he knew as a fact that Sister Claire could quote large passages of the Bible verbatim, which meant that he'd have to make certain that all his *t*'s were crossed and his *i*'s dotted or they'd nail him.

Meanwhile, the KitchenAid mixer had begun to hum. Was

that chocolate he smelled? Perhaps a cake was in the offing for tonight's supper. They hadn't had a chocolate cake since Father Dennis had left. He sure could make a mean triple-layer chocolate cake.

Thoughts of his young assistant made him realize how much he had missed his company these past few weeks. Father Dennis had been called by Father McCarthy, the archdiocese's financial officer. The young priest had been temporarily reassigned while Father McCarthy's assistant recuperated from a broken collarbone. An eighty-five-year-old parishioner had backed over him in the cathedral's parking lot a few weeks ago.

Father James was still rather mystified as to why Father McCarthy had chosen Father Dennis to replace him. Surely there must have been better choices. Father McCarthy had a penchant for order and liked to work with figures, while Father Dennis was incredibly disorganized and had trouble balancing a checkbook.

Strange and mysterious are the ways of the Lord and the church, Father James mused. It would be even stranger if Father Dennis made it through the three-month assignment. The young cleric called almost every night, sounding like a child sent away to camp who was suffering from homesickness.

A knock at his study door rerouted his thoughts.

"Come in."

"Lunch will be ready in about ten minutes," Mrs. Norris announced.

Behind closed eyes, he could feel her giving his study the once-over.

"I see the hymnals are still sitting here unopened. You haven't called Ruth Henderson and tried to smooth this over, now have you?"

"I'm waiting for the right moment," he lied. Ruth and two

other women were protesting the purchase. They preferred the old hymnals.

"Right moment, my foot. You're just afraid to face her. Admit it."

"Why does everything have to be met with controversy?" he challenged. "We're just changing the hymnals . . . same songs, new cover. Why does it have to be such a big deal? It's not like I'm changing the order of mass."

"Ruth says if you replace the old hymnals, she and her sister will refuse to sing."

"*And the Lord shall turn all things toward good,*" he quoted happily. The Henderson sisters were tone-deaf.

Mrs. Norris was still standing over him, so he asked, "Is there something else?"

"You look terrible."

"Thank you," he said, with a sharp edge to his voice.

Why did people think they could make any comment they pleased to a priest? At a wedding last month, a guest had asked him, "Whatever happened to all the good priests?"

"You still have trouble getting to sleep?" she asked.

"Some." He refrained from adding that if she would go away, he might be able to catch a few winks.

"How much sleep did you get last night?"

"An hour or so."

The noon whistle sounded.

"You can't survive on an hour's worth of sleep," she said as though only an idiot would try. "You know, insomnia can be a sign of a more serious illness. My cousin Fremont once ignored a ringing in his ears for months. When he finally got around to visiting the doctor, they discovered a brain tumor. He was dead within the month."

That was a cheery thought. Now, what was she doing? He opened one eye a crack. Darn. She was straightening up his office, which meant that for the next week, he wouldn't be able to find a thing. Last week she had organized his desk. It had taken him the better part of an afternoon to track down the book he had been reading. She had placed it back on the bookshelf. It was the last place he had thought to look. Of course, it was his office and he had every right to ask her to leave it alone, but was it worth risking her ire with lunch in the making?

He felt a sigh building in his chest. It was now officially past his lunch hour, and he felt it unfair to have to deal with Mrs. Norris on an empty stomach.

"Shouldn't you set up for lunch?"

She remained rooted. "Why don't you give Doc Hammon a call?"

"I don't want to bother him. He's got enough really sick patients to worry about. My problem can wait."

"No, it can't," she said firmly.

All hopes of taking a little nap were now gone. He sat up. "Any chance of lunch being served anytime soon?"

"Wash up and I'll put it on the table. And while you're eating, I'll call Doc's office and set up an appointment for this afternoon."

"I'm not sure I'm free this afternoon." He hated it when she tried to take over his life.

"You are. I looked in your daybook."

Father James rolled down his sleeves.

"I wouldn't be too concerned about your insomnia," Doc Hammon said. "Blood pressure, heart rate are all good. But since you're here, I might as well draw some blood. It's been a while since we've checked your cholesterol," he said, referring to the priest's chart.

Darn Mrs. Norris! He hated blood tests. The results were never in his favor. Why did he let Mrs. Norris rule his life?

"My guess is your insomnia is caused by stress. You've been under a lot of pressure lately. That coupled with the added duties you've taken on with Father Dennis away. It happens."

"And what's the cure? I feel like the walking dead," he had to admit, thankful that his housekeeper wasn't around to hear.

"I could give you a prescription for Restoril. It's a mild sleeping pill, but to be honest with you, Jim, I'd rather you try to get past this on your own. Once you start on sleeping pills, it becomes all too easy to rely on them."

Father James watched him scribble something in his chart.

"Any updates on the Gallaghers?" he asked, even though he had spoken with Mike earlier this morning.

Doc removed his reading glasses and rubbed the space between his eyes. "I'm releasing Rodney tomorrow. The frostbite has disappeared. Must be all those prayers that are going up around town."

"And Dexter?"

"No improvement, but then to be honest, I'm not expecting any."

"We're still praying for a miracle," Father James added quietly.

"You'd better step them up. I don't know how much longer the hospital will be willing to keep him on life support."

Chapter Five

ﬡﬠ

Morning mass had ended and parishioners filed out, their voices filling the sanctuary with the easy chatter of friends. Normally Doc's voice would have been among them, asking about Mrs. Norris's arthritis or joking with Timothy about one of his outfits. Last week he had shown up in a pair of black-and-white checked pants, a seventies floral shirt, and army boots.

But this morning there was only One whose company he sought. The battery of tests he had taken over the last two weeks had come back. Three main arteries to his heart were blocked. He'd need a triple bypass.

Doc slid back in the pew. He had no one else but himself to blame. Instead of consuming two grilled cheese sandwiches at a clip, or those porterhouse steaks he favored, he should have paid heed to the advice so often given to his patients—a low-fat, high-fiber diet. More exercise. Sure, he liked to walk, but that was hardly the aerobic activity that the Heart Association recommended.

He leaned his head back against the pew and stared at the ceiling. Had he really thought he was immune to heart disease? He was fifty-seven years old. His father had died at the age of fifty-five of a heart attack, which meant that he was genetically predisposed to heart disease.

Of all the times to take sick, he thought. Who were the Gallaghers going to look to for counsel? This was hardly the time to ask them to rely on the advice of strangers. And what about all his other patients? Fred Campbell was sinking quickly into the black abyss of Alzheimer's. Who was going to convince Arlene that it would be best to place him in a nursing home?

If only he could have found someone he trusted to take over his practice while he was away, but the search had proven fruitless. It seemed there weren't any physicians who wanted to practice medicine in the country.

His eyes fell to Saint Anthony's statue. He and the saint had shared a special bond since he was a young child. How many times had he invoked his intercession on his behalf? Hundreds? Thousands? And each time, things had just sort of worked out. In fact, as a young doctor, he had credited Saint Anthony's intercession in helping him pass his medical boards on the first try.

Doc made his way up the aisle, digging into his pants pocket for some loose change to light a candle. Saint Anthony was the saint of miracles. Maybe he might conjure up another one on behalf of his patients.

He touched a long taper onto a lighted candle, waited until

the flame caught, and lighted another. Watching the yellow orb of light begin to grow, he began to pray.

"Well, dear friend, I need your help once again. Please lend your prayers with mine in asking the Father to send someone with a compassionate heart to take care of my patients while I'm away. I know it will take a miracle, but, after all, you are the saint of miracles."

CRASH!!!

"Sorry about that, Doc," George said, kicking to one side the toolbox that had landed on the marble floor.

"Good God, what is that smell?" Doc asked, backing away.

"That? I was wading around Mildred Dunlop's basement. Her water heater exploded and took out a whole shelf of her pickled cabbage.

"So, you finished up here? I gotta move him," George said, indicating the statue. "That wall behind him needs to come down. A pipe's busted."

"Sure, let me get out of your way," Doc said, high-stepping over the toolbox. Halfway down the aisle he stopped.

"Hey, George?" he called, his voice echoing in the empty sanctuary.

He looked up.

"Be careful with him, will you?" Doc said.

"Don't worry, Doc. Ted's on his way over." Ted was George's new assistant. "We're moving him into the supply closet. Nothing will happen to him in there."

Nothing good ever comes from doing favors for women and dogs, George later remarked to the state trooper who hauled him off to jail.

After Saint Anthony's statue had been safely moved, George

sent Ted along to another job while he went to get some breakfast. All he'd had to eat that morning was a piece of toast and a cup of instant coffee. Right about now, he could go for something more substantial, like a plate of eggs, a small stack of blueberry pancakes, a side of bacon, and some of Harry's home fries.

He had just slid onto his favorite stool, and Wendy had begun to pour his coffee into a mug that bore a picture of a cow, when his cell phone went off.

"What's that awful smell?" Wendy asked, sniffing the air.

George acted as though he hadn't a clue and answered his phone. It was Ted.

"Mrs. Schoonmaker's water heater broke down," Ted told him. "Same problem as the others. The heating element is burnt out."

George swore, right there in public.

Sister Bernadette, who had come to pick up an order of cinnamon buns for this afternoon's bingo game, gasped and made the sign of the cross.

"Sorry, Sister."

That was the third heating unit to give out in the last couple of weeks, and each had the same problem—a defective heating element. He had called the company and asked for replacements. A fat lot of good that had done him. The original company had since been taken over by new owners, and their policy was not to give refunds on anything manufactured before their takeover. End of story. And wouldn't you know it, every dash darn one of the heaters that were defective bore a stamp from before that date. So what could he do but replace them out of his own pocket? His reputation was on the line, and Mrs. Schoonmaker's water heater was number thirteen.

Blasted darn @#%&* company!

He polished off his breakfast in less than ten minutes, seemingly incognizant of the fact that when he had arrived, there had been a line of customers seated alongside him, and now there were none.

"How much do I owe you?" George asked Wendy, fumbling for his wallet.

"Four eighty-five and a can of air freshener," she said without missing a beat.

"Cute," George said, tossing a five-dollar bill on the counter. "Keep the change."

He headed straight over to see Father James, who had a New York lawyer friend, hoping that he might know something about getting this rotten company to make good on all those heaters. But Father James was out so he left a message on his desk and headed back outside. When he was halfway to his truck, Mrs. Norris called from the back porch.

"George. I have an errand I need you to run." Bundled in a cardigan sweater, she trudged down the driveway, hopscotching her way around puddles and slush. "Drop this off at Ethel's," she said, handing him a shopping bag.

It was heavy, so he looked inside. "What's in here?"

"Wine. I'm cleaning out the pantry. Father Dennis loves to cook with it and has open bottles stashed everywhere. Since he's gone, I thought it was a perfect time to get rid of them. I've about had it with him repeatedly setting my stove on fire with those fancy wine sauces he likes to make. So when Ethel called and asked if I had any wine laying around that she might use, I thought I'd send her over the stash." She tightened the sweater around her neck. "The temperature is dropping. I'm going back inside before I catch my death. Now, you hurry along, George, and don't dawdle. Ethel is waiting on you."

She hurried back toward the house, shouting over her shoulder, "And take a bath when you get home. You smell worse than a dead dog."

"Dead dog, huh?" he said, feeling more put upon by the moment. If it weren't for her johnnycakes he'd tell her a thing or two.

He opened the van's door and groaned. Where the heck was he supposed to put this stuff? The van was packed to the gills. He managed to stuff a line of used dryer hose behind the passenger seat, which left room to wedge the shopping bag on the floor between his lunch box and a box of elbow joints, but in the end, only three bottles fit. Great. Now what? Finally he decided to place the bag on the passenger seat and tuck an old sweatshirt around it. He'd have to be careful not to hit any bumps.

Heading over to Ethel's on the other side of town was going to make him late. He was scheduled to meet a contractor over in Woodstock about installing bathrooms in a new development just outside of town. But with any luck, Route 7 would be free of traffic, and he'd sail right over there.

As he suspected, Ethel's driveway was a sheet of ice. She refused to sand it. "It's not good for Honey's paws," she insisted.

Through the intercession of Saint Christopher, he managed to park the van without incident, but gazing out the window, he let loose another round of profanity. The pathway toward the back door hadn't been sanded either. He beeped the horn. He wasn't risking his neck on that ice skating rink. The only response, however, was Honey, who came bounding through the hedges and jumped up on the door. Blast! Where was that woman? He was going to be late.

"Get down, you dog!" he yelled, lowering his window. But Honey's greeting only grew more enthusiastic.

Great! He had half a mind just to drop the bag here on the

driveway and take off. Only thoughts of Mrs. Norris's wrath stopped him from putting that plan in action.

"Get back!" he shouted to Honey, edging out of the driver's seat. He reached across the seat and pulled out the shopping bag, then, walking as gingerly as possible, made his way toward the back door.

Honey thought this good sport and kept blocking his path.

"Go away," he said, trying to balance the shopping bag and avoid the icy patches while fending her off.

But Honey couldn't contain herself. A guest had arrived, and she hadn't yet received an official welcome. That was totally unacceptable. Suddenly, with a quick shake of her tail, she jumped on him and began to cover his face with wet kisses.

"Get down, you crazy mutt!"

But there was no stopping her as the pair crashed to the ground, wine spilling in every direction.

The back door creaked open.

"George Benson!" Ethel screamed. "What do you think you're doing? Is that wine that you're letting Honey lick off your jacket? Don't you know that's not good for dogs?"

George was about as muffed as a man could be by the time he pulled onto Route 7. Blasted dogs and churchwomen! His jacket was ruined and now, along with the smell of rotting cabbage and pine spray, he smelled like a winery.

Suddenly he felt the weight of the black cloud that had tagged him for weeks come crashing down. What was going on lately? Exploding water heaters. Crazed dogs. Had someone put a curse on him? It seemed that every time he turned around another disaster fell out of the sky.

Take last weekend, for example. It was one of those rare

warm March days, and he decided to take his morning cup of coffee out to the back deck. Halfway between the house and the back railing, his foot went right through one of the planks. He called Chester to come survey the damage.

"It's dry rot," Chester told him, kneeling down to examine the boards.

"Can't you just patch it?" he asked hopefully.

"If one board's rotted through, chances are the entire structure is unsound. The deck will have to be replaced."

"So how much is that going to cost me?"

"About fifteen hundred dollars."

Ouch!

George drove the back roads barely conscious of the scenery. He was wondering why his world had taken this sudden downturn and what he could do to undo all this bad luck. By the time he had reached the intersection of Route 202 and Route 7 he had slid into a full-blown state of depression, which was probably why he sailed right through the four-way stop sign.

Minutes later, a state cruiser's flashing lights shone in his rearview mirror.

"I can't believe this!" George pulled over and hung his head over the steering wheel. Just what he needed. A ticket.

It seemed to George that it took the officer an inordinately long time to make it toward the van. Finally he sauntered over and stood staring at his ticket book while he asked to see George's license and registration.

"Something wrong, Officer?" George asked, pretending he had done nothing wrong. He passed the documents through the opened window.

"You missed a stop sign back there," the officer told him, studying George's photo.

"I did?"

The officer frowned and leaned in toward the van. "Have you been drinking, sir?"

"Drinking? Who, me? No. I haven't been drinking."

"What's that on your jacket?"

George looked down. "Oh, that? I can explain . . ."

"Is that an open bottle of wine I see on the passenger seat?"

George looked to his right. Oh, no . . . he had forgotten about that bottle. "I can explain that too," he began.

"Sir, step out of the van, sir."

"You don't understand. I would never drink and drive. Why, I'm a member of Saint Cecilia's over in Dorsetville. You see, I was asked to deliver some open bottles of wine to one of our parishioners. She was having company tonight and—"

"Get out of the car, sir," the officer repeated with a sharp edge to his voice.

"Here, I can prove it."

A church bulletin was lying on the cab's floor. His name was listed as a member of the parish council. That should straighten things out. He bent down to grab it.

Uncertain of his intentions, the trooper jumped back, pulled out his revolver, and aimed it right at George's head.

"GET OUT OF THE VAN NOW WITH YOUR HANDS BEHIND YOUR HEAD!"

George prayed that no one would recognize him as he and Father Keene made their way through the state troopers' parking lot. All he wanted to do was to go home and take a shower. His head was pounding. What a day!

The officer had issued him a five-hundred-dollar fine for driving with an open bottle of alcohol, and his license had been suspended. He was due in court next week to plead his case be-

fore a district judge. But in the meantime, his van had been im-
pounded and he had been told that if he wished to retrieve it,
he would have to return with someone who had a valid driver's
license and who could drive it home for him.

Now, how the heck was he supposed to carry on his business if he couldn't drive? he wanted to know.

"So, who's driving us back to town?" he asked the elderly
priest. Father Keene's license had been revoked ten years ago
when he had nearly run down a herd of Joe Platt's cows.

"Not to worry, laddie. I have everything covered."

Why did that statement bother him? George wondered.
He had only called the retirement home in hopes of catching
Chester Platt, who he knew was finishing up some renovation
work there for the nuns.

"Chester left about an hour ago," Father Keene had told
him. "Is there something I can help you with?"

After swearing the priest to secrecy, George told him about
his arrest.

"Not to worry, son," he said in his lilting Irish accent. "I'll
find a way to get you home." He had arrived forty minutes
later.

Father Keene took a right at the far end of the parking lot
and headed toward the battered station wagon that belonged
to the nuns. George should have felt the first inkling of alarm
when he noticed it parked at a rather strange angle. But by now,
his observational skills were below par, having been anesthe-
tized by the day's events.

"I borrowed the good sister's car," Father Keene said matter-
of-factly, removing a set of car keys from his coat pocket.

"You mean you drove over here by yourself? Holy shi—"
Could this day possibly get any worse?

"We have to hurry," Father Keene told him. "Sister Bernadette will be finishing up bingo shortly. She doesn't know I took it."

Resigned to the course of events that continued to spin out of his control, George slid into the passenger side, then waited for Father Keene to maneuver himself behind the wheel. George watched with a sinking feeling as the priest perched on top of a thick copy of *The Catechism of the Catholic Church* in order to see above the steering wheel.

George watched hopelessly as Father Keene started the engine with a roar and a thick cloud of white smoke enveloped the car. Then, turning to look over the backseat, Father Keene gave it the gas. The car lurched forward, coming within inches of a tree.

"Reverse. Put it in reverse," George shouted, his fingernails embedded in the dashboard. It would be a blooming miracle if they made it home in one piece.

"So, what were you in for?" Father Keene asked, finally maneuvering out of the parking lot and onto the main road.

"It's a long story. You know, I never had these kinds of problems when I was a Methodist." George was a recent convert. Maybe that was it. Maybe he should have stayed a Methodist. "Watch out for that stop sign. Stop sign! STOP SIGN!"

Father Keene hit the brakes with both feet. George slid to the floor.

"Yes, it does seem that sometimes we Catholics are put to the test more than other denominations," Father Keene agreed. The speedometer never went beyond twenty-five miles per hour, but the priest was oblivious to the stream of cars that were collecting behind him.

"Someone should have told me that before I signed up," George quipped, this time making certain his seat belt was fastened.

"Well, there's no undoing it now, my boy. Once a Catholic, always a Catholic."

Ethel chopped, minced, and diced her way through several Hail Marys and Our Fathers, prayers being lifted up for the Gallaghers. Her heart was heavy with compassion for the young family. The boys had once been in her catechism class.

But the Gallaghers weren't the only ones that tugged at her heartstrings. She was also deeply concerned for the Campbells.

Fred was growing more unmanageable every day, yet Arlene refused to place him in a nursing home. Both Ethel and Harriet urged her to reconsider. The burden of Fred's daily care was taking its toll. But she refused to heed their advice and was duty bound to plow along, even if it meant risking her own health. Last visit to Doc's, her blood pressure registered dangerously high.

It was hard watching from the sidelines as friends and neighbors suffered, which was why Ethel was so thankful for the company that was coming to dinner tonight. Preparations helped to refocus her mind onto other things and lighten her heavy heart.

Mother Superior and Father Keene were due at five-thirty, and she knew that they prided themselves on being punctual. Sam and Harriet would arrive later for dessert. She glanced up at the clock above the sink. It was already nearing one o'clock, which didn't give her much time to prepare the meal and clean up all of Honey's hairs, a must when entertaining Catholic clergy. The one time she had forgotten to vacuum the sofa (which Honey used as her personal daybed) Father James went home looking as though he had grown a fur coat.

She quickly threw together Honey's lunch. Two cups of Pro

Plan, half a cup of diced chicken, and a dribble of chicken broth. Ethel gave it a last stir, then set it on the linoleum floor. The retriever gobbled it down as though she hadn't eaten for weeks, then collapsed underneath the kitchen table to take a nap.

Meanwhile, Ethel got busy gathering the ingredients for Father Keene's favorite dessert, cherry cheesecake. When her husband was alive, she baked often, but now only when company was coming. She had forgotten how much she enjoyed baking and found herself humming as she followed the recipe card.

Preheat oven to 300 degrees. Empty one package of yellow cake mix in a large bowl, reserving 1 cup. Add 3 tablespoons of vegetable oil and 1 egg (slightly beaten), and press the crust evenly along the bottom and ¾ up the sides of a greased 9" × 12" pan. Mix with an electric mixer: 2 (8 oz.) packages of cream cheese, ½ cup sugar, 3 eggs, until smooth. Add 3 tablespoons lemon juice, 3 teaspoons vanilla extract, 1½ cup milk, and the reserved 1 cup of cake mix. Beat until smooth. Pour into the pan. Bake 40–50 minutes or until done. Cool. Top with two cans of cherry pie filling.

A large picture window on the south side of the kitchen faced a small meadow that gave rise to the mountain range. It was teaming with wildlife and a constant source of entertainment. Even Honey enjoyed looking out, as was evidenced by the constant nose prints on the glass.

This winter had been especially hard on the deer and other small creatures that lived in the forest. Supplies were low, which often forced them to forage along her back property line. Some folks thought them a nuisance, especially the deer, which stripped every green plant and snipped off the tops of crocus and tulips at the rate of a buzz saw. But she didn't mind. She loved all of God's creatures and placed salt licks for the deer at the edge of the woods, hung suet for the birds, and kept a bin filled with vegetable peelings for the raccoons—which, unfortunately, the skunks had also discovered, so a close watch had to be kept on Honey after dusk.

It was late afternoon by the time she finished the cake and cleared the sink of dirty dishes. The meadow and pond lay quiet, poised between daylight and dusk. It was still light enough, however, to discern a cottontail's fresh footprints and those of squirrels, possum, and deer, which created a patchwork design running the length and width of the snow-covered field.

Just beyond the small pond to the east of her property, wheat-colored remains of various wild grasses and dried wildflower stalks sprouted out here and there. The previous summer they had filled the back fields in a profusion of color, a symphony of movement. Now they bowed like old men huddled underneath a thick covering of snow and ice.

She decided to serve dinner boardinghouse style here in the kitchen. They would serve themselves out of ironstone bowls, pour drinks from an old milk pitcher. Mother Superior and Father Keene were dear friends. No need for pretensions. Besides, Father James had once said that he wished more parishioners would treat clergy more like family. Simple meals and good conversations, not fancy formal dinners, were what they really craved.

Sam and Harriet would be arriving later for dessert. They, too, preferred the coziness of the buttercream walls and the soft calico curtains to the staunch formality of the dining room, with its Chippendale mahogany table that had once belonged to Ethel's mother-in-law.

The kitchen was Ethel's favorite room in the house, perhaps because, like most women, she spent the majority of her time there. No matter who came to visit, they always seemed to end up in this room. There was just something comforting about this hub of the house with its golden oak cabinets, the smell of spices, and meals simmering on the back of the stove.

By late afternoon, all was ready for her guests. She opened the oven door and was greeted with the smell of beef tenderloin in rich dark gravy laced with wine, sweet carrots, onions, and parsnips. She inhaled deeply. The flaky pastry that covered the dish was browning nicely. She lowered the temperature and smiled in satisfaction, envisioning the joy on Father Keene's and Mother Superior's faces as they took their first bite.

The kitchen had grown dark. Ethel switched on the overhead light. Everything was ready. Friends would be here in another hour. All that was left to do was to make a salad.

She pulled out a kitchen chair and sat down to catch her breath, just as the sun began to dip behind the mountains. Night was falling. Her mind wandered over the meadow, trying to catch one last glimpse of the landscape before it was shrouded in darkness.

Chapter Six

Doc Hammon had one more phone call to make before he left for the sixty-minute drive to Hartford Hospital, a hospital that specialized in cardiac care. The call was to a friend, Dr. Morris Leventhal, chief of surgery at Boston General, whom he hadn't seen in several years.

"Well, if it isn't a voice from the past! You still practicing snake oil medicine up in the wilds of—what was the name of that town?"

"Dorsetville. Yes, I'm still here," he said, laughing.

"Excuse me," Morris said as he spoke to his secretary. "Sorry about the interruption. I have a budget meeting in about twenty minutes."

"Then I won't keep you. I need a special favor."

"Anything for an old friend."

"I'm scheduled for surgery and I need someone to take over my practice when I'm gone. I was hoping that you might know of someone."

"I take it you don't have an assistant?" He heard Morris lean back in his chair.

"The practice isn't big enough."

"Gee, Jack, as much as I'd like to help, I really can't think of anyone off the top of my head. But, tell you what. Let me ask around. Who knows, I might scrape up someone who doesn't mind making house calls in a horse-drawn carriage."

Doc laughed. "I appreciate your help."

"When are you scheduled for surgery?"

"Tomorrow."

"That doesn't give me much time, but I'll do my best. Meanwhile, what's the name of that saint you were always invoking in med school?"

"Saint Anthony."

"Maybe he can help you find a replacement," Morris teased.

"I've already asked him."

Four miles out of town, on a hilltop that rose above the meadow to Platt's farm, a tall, broad-shouldered young man stood gazing down at the town below. As shadows thickened, tiny orbs of light pinpricked the darkness, reminding him of a galaxy of stars.

From this vantage point, it was easy to make out the band of buildings strung along the town's main street. There was Dinova's Grocery Store, which he knew would remain open for several more hours so folks coming home from work could pick up their orders. And when the last customer had been served, Gus Dinova, who had inherited the store from his father along with his love for Italian opera, would drop off a package of Social Teas for Fred Campbell on his way home. Arlene had left them behind when she came in earlier with Ethel.

Down the street from Dinova's, at Secondhand Rose, a crate of dishes was being delivered. He smiled just thinking about the treasures soon to be discovered, packed inside.

And then as he thought about all the other good people who lived in the town, he heard the soft peal of Saint Cecilia's church bells. He closed his eyes and let the sweet music fill his soul. The sound sent his thoughts back to that night two thousand years ago when heaven's bells chimed in commemoration of Jesus' birth.

Darkness was quickly descending on the small village like a curtain closing at the end of a play. A strong breeze blew down the mountainside and the wind whispered something in his ear. He nodded and then, placing his hands inside his large sleeves, he started down the hillside toward the town that had beckoned.

Shirley Olsen had worked as Doc's office manager–receptionist–accountant and sounding board for twenty-five years and had seen him through flu epidemics that had kept him going steady for nearly six weeks; insurance premium increases that had Doc wondering if he would have to get a night job; births, deaths, good patients and bad; his father's death and, later, his mother's cancer.

She knew when he was worried about a patient before he knew it himself, and when he was about to throw one of his yearly tirades over a health insurance company's refusal to pay certain claims. She knew when he was so tired that he was about to fall down, and when his blood pressure was up again. She knew him inside and out, which was why she had known something was wrong for weeks, way before he brought her into his office to deliver the news.

"I need a triple bypass," he said after they were seated. "I'll be leaving tomorrow morning for Hartford Hospital."

Hot tears sprang to her eyes. No words would come.

"It's going to be all right," he said soothingly. Shirley was like a sister, and he hated to see her so upset.

"You promise?" she said, even though she was acutely aware it was a promise he really couldn't make.

Doc laughed and told her that he'd do his best to comply, adding, "You may have to close the office. I tried to find a re-placement but there aren't a lot of doctors who care to try their hand at country living."

"It's their loss," she said, and meant it. "You just take care of yourself. I'll manage things around here until you get back."

"I'm sure you can," he said, then slid back in his chair. "This is a darn inconvenient time to have to take off."

She knew he was thinking about the Gallaghers. The whole town was concerned, but he shouldn't be centered on that right now. He needed to get well.

"Listen, I know that this might not be the best time to take a sick leave, but there's always going to be a health crisis of one sort or the other in this town. Right now, you have to concen-trate on taking care of yourself and getting well."

"Yeah, but—"

"No buts about it. Think on this. If something happens to you, who will take care of all these people? As you've discovered, there's not a long line of doctors waiting to take over your practice. At least, not at the salary you take home, and I should know. I write out your checks."

Even though all the appointments had been canceled, Shirley came into the office, just as she had done for several decades. She needed to be available to direct any patient calls.

She did what she always did first thing in the morning. She put her purse in the bottom right-hand drawer, took off her coat, and went to make a cup of tea. While she waited for water to boil, she fed Tunes. She had volunteered to cat-sit while Doc and Joan were away.

Shirley glanced over at the wall clock. Doc should be arriving in Hartford about now. She tried not to think what might happen to this town if Doc didn't make it through the surgery. He was more than the town's physician. To many, he was a dear and treasured friend.

She didn't know of one person who wasn't indebted to him for one thing or another. The Kilbourne girls would have lost their eyesight if Doc hadn't persisted and found a clinic that could treat their rare eye disease.

The Nelson baby would have died of congenital heart failure if Doc hadn't stepped in. The family had no insurance, so he had paid their expenses out of his own pocket. The Nelsons had been paying off that debt, $10 a week, for the last fifteen years. Their son, Charlie, had just made linebacker for the high school football team.

Doc was also known for having a heart bigger than the state of Texas. Every year he collected toys for kids he knew whose family couldn't afford gifts, and even though he seldom had enough to cover his own bills, it never stopped him from being generous. As Doc always said, "Give with your heart and God will work out the finances." And somehow he always did.

She poured milk into her tea and settled back behind her desk. Tunes wandered in and out of Doc's office, then came to perch alongside her chair, his yellow eyes seeming to ask, "Where did he go?" It brought tears to her eyes.

"You'd better keep your promise to me, Jack Hammon," she said out loud, scratching Tunes behind the ears. Then turning toward the cat, she added, "The good book says, 'Where two or more are gathered, there I am in the midst.' I know that you love him just as much as I do, so as I see it, that qualifies you as my prayer partner."

And so the cat and woman began their prayer.

Dear Lord, watch over him. I don't have to tell you how much he's needed around here. Send a host of angels before him to keep him safe, and send him back to us whole.

And if you could, please send a doctor to watch over his patients. I know that would give him so much comfort, knowing that they were being cared for.

She hadn't heard anyone walk in and jumped when a man's voice called her name. Sliding the glass partition to one side, she asked, "May I help you?"

"My name is Dr. Nathan Noiyst. I've been sent to take over Doc Hammon's practice while he's gone."

Shirley looked down at Tunes. "You're some powerful prayer partner."

As Doc Hammon was being wheeled into surgery, prayers were going up all over Dorsetville.

"Lord have mercy," one woman said to her best friend. "I swear, if one more person in this town needs prayer, I may never get up off my knees.

"I wonder, with Doc gone, who'll take care of the Gallagher boys. I hear Rodney is being released this afternoon. Margaret Norris is taking care of him during the day while the parents are at the hospital."

"Poor Lorraine. They say she hasn't left Dexter's side since the accident."

"I hear he's not doing well. In fact, my niece—you know, the one who works on the maternity ward—says she heard that they want to take him off life support."

"It's going to be real hard on the Gallaghers without Doc Hammon."

"I heard that when Doc broke the news to Lorraine, she cried so hard that he had to sedate her."

The world outside Dexter's hospital room had ceased to exist for Lorraine Gallagher. Night turned to day, visitors came and went, but she hardly noticed. Nurses brought trays of food, but they went untouched.

Even the mention of Rodney's name brought little response. Although she loved both sons equally, right now Dexter's needs took precedence. She didn't care what they said. She knew he would recover. He had to.

She ran a gentle hand along her son's soft cheek. How small and pale he looked, so unlike the robust boy who had romped and played and caused all kinds of mischief from one end of Dorsetville to the other. Even through the veil of grief, a semblance of a smile surfaced as she remembered some of his antics. The time that he slipped his pet snake inside Mother

Superior's desk drawer. The day that he snatched the nuns' underwear from their clothesline and stuffed it inside Father Dennis's car. The poor priest had been red-faced as he handed Sister Claire a brown paper bag filled with their unmentionables.

At the time, she had wondered if she would ever make it through his childhood. Now she wondered, looking down at his motionless form, if she would make it in a world without him. As soon as the thought emerged, she chided herself. NO! NO! NO! He would get better. He would!

If only he would open his eyes, call out her name. She took his small, childlike hand into hers and brought it up to her cheek, kissing each finger softly.

"My baby," she whispered. "My, sweet, sweet boy, please come back to me. Come back to me now."

Dexter paused. Was that his mother's voice he had just heard? But it sounded as if it were so far away.

He turned slowly, searching the meadow for his mother's bright smile, her opened arms, but she was not there. A soft breeze, like a giant hand, moved across the grass, but it was empty except for Jennie.

Normally Dexter didn't like girls much, but Jennie was different. He watched her now, standing among an assortment of forest animals—raccoons, bobcats, possum, and bears. They were taking food from her hand.

"Would you like to try?" she asked, extending an empty palm that magically filled with feed.

It was one of the things about this place that amazed him. Whatever you needed or thought about just appeared. It was so cool.

"Sure," he said, ambling over, surprised to find that he wasn't the least bit frightened by the brown bear or the bobcat that brushed up against his pants leg. He reached down and ran his hand across their fur. Both rolled over onto their backs, lifting their paws high up into the air as though they wanted to play.

"Jennie! Dexter!"

He followed the sound. A group of kids were standing on the far side of a stream.

"Want to play softball?" they called, indicating a baseball diamond that sparkled under the brilliant light. "We could sure use some extra players."

"It will be fun, Dexter," Jennie coaxed, taking his hand. "That is, if you're ready to cross over now."

Dexter looked at the stream separating the meadow from the field. "I don't know," he hedged. Something was holding him back. He shook his hand free.

"You can't stay here much longer," she told him, walking toward the stream. "Very soon, you'll have to make a decision, to stay or to go back."

Chapter Seven

Mrs. *Norris* stepped out of the second-floor elevator and studied the visitor's card given her downstairs. It read *Room 205*. Rodney was being discharged at eleven, and she had offered to watch him until his father got home this evening.

According to the sign posted on the opposite wall, she needed to take a right. Slipping the paper inside her purse, she headed in that direction, completely unaware that the boy she had come to retrieve was hiding behind the potted palm.

Rodney waited until she was safely out of sight and made a mad dash into the elevator seconds before the doors slid shut. A tall bearded man who smelled of garlic and was holding a bouquet of flowers smiled at him. Rodney gave him a leery look and edged toward the rear of the car.

As he watched the display panel directly above the doors count off the ascending floors, he tried to formulate some kind of plan. Up until now, his only mission had been to see Dexter. He hadn't given much thought to how that was to be done. He knew only that he had to see Dexter before Mrs. Norris took him home.

He had grown tired of adults refusing to give him a straight answer. The nurses changed the subject. Father James said Dexter was "doing as well as could be expected," and his dad dished out a really lame story about Dexter having gotten a highly contagious cold from his plunge through the ice and being in isolation. *Bullwinkle* was what he had to say about that! Something was wrong with Dexter. He could feel it, and he was not leaving this place until he found out what!

Two more floors and he'd be there. His heartbeat quickened and he began to fidget. The bearded man turned to stare. Rodney reined himself in. He figured he had one shot at finding Dexter, just one, and he couldn't chance this guy asking questions or getting him thrown off.

He wasn't sure what was wrong with Dex, but one thing was certain, his brother needed him. He could feel it, so he'd better not screw this up.

The man got off on the fifth floor. Dexter was on the sixth. Rodney's eyes were glued to the display panel. It seemed as though the needle would never move up that final notch. Just when he was convinced that something was drastically wrong, it clicked into place, accompanied by the sound of a bell, and the doors slid open.

He hit the Stop button and peeked out like a marine to study the terrain. To the left was a long corridor that ended at a large bank of doors above which was posted a sign reading *Surgery*. That wasn't it.

He looked to the right. There was a small vestibule with a bank of chairs and two large metal doors. The sign on these doors read, *Intensive Care Unit. Ring Buzzer for Admittance. No One Under 18 Allowed*. Bingo! He had called the main operator and asked for his brother's room. They had told him that he was in the ICU, but nothing more. "I'm sorry, young man," the lady had said. "We are not allowed to give out information about our patients."

He swung back inside the elevator to think, hoping that no one would come along and ask him why he was holding up the car.

Dexter was inside, but how was he supposed to get in?

From down the hall he heard a steady *clack, clack,* the sound a rubber wheel makes as it glides across the floor. He snuck another peek. A supply cart had been pushed against a far wall near the Intensive Care Unit. Several feet over, a middle-aged woman dressed in a gray uniform, sporting a name tag that identified her as *Maria De Santos, Housekeeping,* was engaged in conversation with a janitor, who was leaning against a dry mop.

"Charlene called in sick again," the woman was saying, in a heavy Spanish accent. "That's the third time this week. Last time she said her car broke down. Oh yeah? Then what was she doing roaming around the mall, I ask you? My sister saw her shopping in Macy's. So here I am, stuck with cleaning Intensive Care again. I hate that unit. It gives me the willies. All those people more dead than alive."

The man leaned in and spoke in a whisper, "I know what you mean. One time, there was this old woman . . ."

What did she mean, more dead than alive? Rodney wondered, and felt the first chill of fear. But there was no time to think about that now. Someway, he had to get in to see Dex.

Then he had an idea. He'd stow away on the supply cart. The woman said she had been called to clean the unit. Brilliant! There was just one drawback. First he'd have to make it past the couple without being tagged.

Dexter had once said that if you're in a place you don't belong and don't want to get snagged, walk with a sense of purpose. "Nobody ever stops a kid if they act as though they know where they're going," he had said.

Okay, brother, I hope you know what you're talking about, Rodney thought, starting down the hall as though he owned the place. Luckily, there was a men's room several yards past the cart, so he acted as though he were headed that way.

It worked like a charm. *Good old Dex!* While the man and the woman were occupied, Rodney slipped unnoticed onto the cart's lower shelf and burrowed himself beneath a pile of crisp white sheets. Then he waited for his ride.

Mike wanted to punch someone or something. The neurologist had just left. The hospital wanted to remove Dexter's life support.

"He's not going to get better," the physician in his spotless lab coat had said. "I know that's hard for you to hear, but that is the fact."

Lorraine's vehement reply sent him scurrying, but not before he hastily added, "We're prepared to seek a court order, if we have to."

Mike walked across the cubicle and slammed his fist against the wall.

"Mike, please," Lorraine pleaded.

"Please what?"

"Stay focused on God's promises, not on what the doctors say," she replied softly.

"Yeah, right." He looked at her as though she were a stranger.

How could she sit there day in and day out and never lose faith? How did she maintain her belief that God would miraculously revive their son? It was unrealistic. It was fanaticism. God didn't care about one small child. If he did, he would never have allowed this to happen in the first place.

Mike was filled with white rage. He needed someone to blame, some way to channel the anger that coursed through his veins like poison.

He hated Doc Hammon for abandoning them. He hated this hospital. He even hated his wife. She was the one to blame for all of this. Why hadn't she forbidden the boys to go skating that day, kept a better eye on them? He watched her now, speaking softly to their son as though he could hear.

He turned toward the window and clutched his head. What was wrong with him? He didn't hate his wife. He loved her, and he wasn't mad at Doc Hammon. It wasn't his fault he had fallen ill. Besides, he really liked his replacement, Dr. Noiyst. In fact, he was the only one who seemed to be able to still Mike's pain. For some unfathomable reason, when he was around, Mike felt hope rekindled. He wished he would walk in now. He was quickly losing all sense of hope.

Mike glanced back at his son. His anger returned. If only Rodney had kept better tabs on his brother. He knew how impulsive Dexter could be. He told his wife that.

She looked at him incredulously. "You're trying to blame Rodney for this?"

"He's the oldest," he replied, coldly.

"By what, two and a half minutes? How does that make a difference?"

"I told Rodney that the temperature had warmed, that the ice was unstable. I warned him to stay away, but did he listen?"

"He's just a child," she reminded him. "For Pete's sake, Mike, have you forgotten that Rodney risked his own life trying to save his brother's?"

"Maybe he should have tried a little harder," Michael shot back without thinking.

"I can't believe you mean that," she gasped.

No, he hadn't meant it, but it was too late. Rodney had slipped unnoticed into the room.

"I'm sorry, Dad," he said, looking small and frightened, tears spilling down his checks.

"Oh, no," Mike groaned. He rushed over to embrace his son, burying his face into his neck. "Don't listen to me, Rodney. I didn't mean what I just said. It's just that . . ." He began to sob. What was wrong with him? How could he have said something so hateful?

"We're very concerned for your brother," Lorraine finished, bending down. He rushed into her arms. She scooped him up and stroked his hair.

"What's wrong with Dex?" he asked softly, glancing past her shoulder.

"He's in a coma," she explained.

"Can I talk to him?"

"Sure you can. But he might not respond."

Rodney cautiously neared the bed. "Hi, Dex. It's me." He waited anxiously, but there was no response. "When will he wake up?"

His dad placed a hand on his shoulder. "We don't know, son. Some of the doctors think that he might never wake up."

"You mean like . . . he might die?" His face filled with fear. No, that couldn't be right. Dexter wasn't supposed to die. They were just kids.

"Yes. I'm sorry, Son," Mike said, drawing him near. He felt Rodney stiffen.

"Mom?" His father had to be wrong.

A look was exchanged between the two parents. Mike seemed to be asking Lorraine to consider what might happen if her miracle never came. He didn't want the boy filled with false hope.

"All of us will die someday, darling," she said, softly.

"No! Not Dex! Not him!" he shouted, shaking his brother's hand. "Wake up, Dex! Wake up!"

"Don't, Rodney. Please," his mom said.

Dexter's hand began to shake, and for a second Rodney thought that he was responding. But then something scary happened. Dexter's body began to tremble violently. Growing stronger and stronger.

"What's wrong with Dex?" He was really frightened now.

Before his mother could answer, a buzzer in the nurses' station sounded. Medical personnel rushed in, took one look at Dexter, and demanded that the family step outside.

"Dexter, come on. Just step over the stream," Jennie instructed. "They're waiting for us on the other side."

Dexter was about to follow when he heard Rodney's voice. It was faint, but he seemed to be telling him to *wake up*. Wake up? He wasn't asleep. He looked around. Where was Rodney anyway? It wasn't like him to lag behind.

"If you don't hurry, you won't be able to play," Jennie said, urging him to follow.

Dexter studied the ball field. It lay just across the stream. He watched the teams begin to line up. They were wearing some really neat uniforms with pinstriping down the side of the pants that flashed like a string of Christmas lights. How cool was that? He sure hoped they had one in his size.

One of the boys put his hands around his mouth like a megaphone and hollered, "Hurry up! We're getting ready to start!"

"Oh, what the heck," he said, walking toward the stream. Rodney could catch up with him later. He didn't want to miss out on the fun.

Rodney was unnaturally quiet on the ride back into Dorsetville as the familiar landscape slid by. Mrs. Norris sensed the boy didn't want to talk. From what she had learned from the medical staff, Dexter wasn't expected to make it through the day.

And while she thought about ways to help soften the boy's heartache, Rodney fought to erase what he had witnessed. Dexter flailing around the bed. The nurse forcing a tongue depressor into his mouth so he wouldn't swallow his tongue. The way they had tied down his feet and hands to the bed.

Rodney swallowed hard, forcing back a sob.

He also couldn't erase what his dad had said about this being his fault. Maybe he was right. If only he had obeyed his dad. His dad did tell him to stay off the ice that day.

And when Dexter had fallen through, maybe he could have tried harder to save him. He cupped a hand underneath his chin and forced back a hot stream of tears. *Dex, what am I going to do if you die?*

They rode in silence for several miles. He was glad that Mrs.

Norris had come to get him; at least she didn't blabber all the time like other old ladies.

Suddenly he remembered the message Dex had given him. What exactly was it? It had something to do with a girl. What was her name? Oh yeah . . .

"Mrs. Norris?"

"Yes, Rodney."

"Who is Jennie?"

Father James hadn't had a restful night's sleep in over a week. He went to bed tired but just couldn't turn his mind off. As soon as his head hit the pillow, a geyser of thoughts would gush forth that no amount of self-will seemed able to stem.

He had tried everything. He prayed, but instead of feeling a gentle peace, he grew increasingly more anxious over the problems of those whom he was lifting up in prayer. Like the Gallaghers.

They certainly had had a close call today. Dexter had gone into convulsions and his heart had stopped. When the neurologist walked in, he gave the order to stop resuscitation. Miraculously, Dr. Noiyst appeared and insisted they continue CPR. Moments later, Dexter was once again brought back from the brink of death.

The episode made him revisit the quandary: Should he prepare the Gallaghers to accept Dexter's death? Was it inevitable, as the neurologists said? Or should he encourage them to have faith in a God who knew no impossibilities?

He wished God would give him a clear directive in this matter, but so far, he had been silent, leaving Father James to rely upon his own deductive faculties, a poor substitution for divine guidance.

The nightstand clock edged toward two. He grabbed a pillow, punched it down, and tried to find a comfortable spot. Nothing, however, felt right. If he didn't get some sleep soon, he would be wasted for tomorrow.

He fluffed more pillows, pulled blankets on, took them off, growing more and more anxious by the minute. He counted backward from one hundred, forced his mind to go blank. Seconds later, new thoughts came rolling in like thunder.

At 3 A.M. he went downstairs and turned the gas on underneath the teakettle. He was desperate enough to try a cup of chamomile tea. Mrs. Norris insisted that it was the only remedy for insomnia. He found the pale blue box next to the can of hot cocoa mix that he would have much preferred.

He made his tea (yellow-colored . . . well, he really didn't want to think that thought through) and headed back upstairs, the ancient floorboards creaking underfoot. How quiet the rectory had become and how unsettling it felt to be alone. Father Dennis was away. Mrs. Norris had left right after dinner.

Until a few months ago, he had enjoyed the company of Stephen Richter. But Stephen had since moved into his own apartment, above one of the stores along Main Street—a temporary move, since he and Valerie Kilbourne were engaged.

Father James leaned against the banister, sipped his tea, and pondered the strange feel of the house. The special warmth and comfort he had always felt were gone. They had left with the people who had shared this space. For the first time he truly understood what parents must feel when their children leave home, or the emptiness associated with widowhood.

He must have eventually fallen asleep. The last time he had glanced at the dial on his clock it had read 3:35. But at 4:09 he was pulled back from a blessed slumber by the shrill ring of the front doorbell. What the blazes?

"Hold on, hold on. I'm coming!" he shouted, slipping into his robe. In his hurry, he managed to lose a slipper underneath the bed.

"Good grief!"

The night visitor had abandoned the door chimes and was now pounding on the front door.

Father James found the lost slipper, and nearly flew down the front staircase. He threw on the porch light.

"Who's there?"

"Mike Gallagher."

He fumbled for the handle. Imagining the worst, his stomach began a free fall.

"I'm so sorry to disturb you, Father," Mike said.

"Dexter . . . is he?"

Mike shook his head, no.

"Thank the Lord! Come in out of the cold." Father James pulled him through the door. The temperature had dropped another ten degrees.

Mike looked as though he had slept in his clothes. His cheeks were bright red orbs. His eyes were swollen from crying, and his face wore the haggard expression of one who has been through a war.

"Come into the kitchen and I'll put on a pot of coffee," Father James offered. "You look like you could use some warming up."

Mike nodded and followed him mutely.

"Take a seat while I wrestle with our new coffeemaker. Mrs. Norris bought it on sale the other day at Filene's, although I don't know for the life of me what was wrong with the old one. At least that one I knew how to run. You need an engineering degree just to turn this darn thing on. But you know women. They like to keep us men on our toes." He was rambling, trying to fill in the silence.

Mike slid into a chair and placed his head in his hands, crying softly. Father James tactfully placed a box of tissues on the table, then went in search of the coffee. Mike would tell him what was wrong when he was ready.

Both the pantry and the cabinets came up empty. Finally he found it at the back of the refrigerator in a clear plastic canister.

That was another thing that mystified him about women. Why couldn't they just leave well enough alone? Coffee manufacturers spent hundreds of thousands of dollars developing the perfect container. He liked the fact that the decaf coffees came in green containers and said *Decaffeinated* and the regular stuff came in cans marked *Regular*. So what made women disregard expensive product research and transfer contents into clear plastic containers that never provided a clue as to what was inside?

He hoped he had chosen the "high-test." Sleep was definitely not an option tonight and he could use a jump start.

Meanwhile his mind raced along like a thoroughbred racehorse. What words of comfort might he offer this young father? Then it came to him. The words Mike had come to hear would not come from him but through him. In the silence of his heart, he surrendered himself fully to the workings of the Holy Spirit, whom Jesus called the Comforter.

Make me an instrument of your peace, he prayed.

The coffeemaker buzzed, indicating it was finished brewing. Through some stroke of luck, he had managed to push all the right buttons. The smell of freshly brewed coffee wafted through the kitchen like incense.

He filled two mugs, handed one to Mike, then pulled out a chair and settled in. For several minutes, the men sat quietly. Finally Mike turned to face him and stated simply, "If this is a test of faith, then I've failed miserably."

Father James was familiar with this line of thinking, which many went through during periods of difficult trials, so he countered with, "Do you think that God has deliberately planned this test so he might prove how much you love him?"

"Isn't that what he did to Job?"

"Are you Job?"

"No, but I thought . . . I thought . . ." He looked at the priest, his face a mix of emotions. "Hell, I don't know what I thought. All I know is that the doctors say my son is brain-dead, and that the only thing keeping him alive is a bunch of machines. And now Rodney thinks this is all his fault."

"Why?"

Mike looked at the priest with intense anguish. "He overheard me say that he should have tried harder to save his brother."

"Oh no . . ."

"I didn't mean it. I was angry. I needed to blame someone, and he just happened to walk in while I was venting."

The priest placed a hand on his shoulder. "You're a good father, Mike. Deep down, Rodney knows that you didn't mean that. If you want, I can talk to him, explain the kind of pressure you're under."

"Thanks, Father, but I'm afraid that he'll never forgive me. I've lost one son. Now I'm afraid I've lost the other." Tears copiously flowed. He turned a troubled face toward Father James and cried in torment, "Where is God in all of this? Where was he when my son fell through the ice? He may not have done this, but he certainly could have prevented it."

Mike looked up at Father James, searching for an answer. "I've tried all of my life to be faithful to God and to the Church. I've been a responsible parent and husband. I've been as trustworthy as I know how with all the talents and resources that God has sent my way."

"I know you have," Father James agreed.

"I don't deserve this. Why is God letting this happen?"

Father James leaned his arms heavily on the worn kitchen table and clasped his hands. "That's one of the most difficult questions to answer, Mike. I wish I could give you a definitive answer, but the truth is . . . I can't."

"Then what good is faith?"

"Faith is by definition the substance of things hoped for and the evidence of things not seen."

"Just believing for belief's sake, is that it?" Mike asked with a flash of anger. "That doesn't wash. What kind of God would expect me to believe in his goodness without evidence of that love?"

Father James paused, knowing the answer to that question could be accepted only with an open heart, and right now Mike's was tightly shut.

"Isn't it a miracle that Rodney fell through the ice near the exact same spot as Dexter, yet he didn't drown?" he asked him. "Some would say that it was God's grace that spared him."

Mike thought about that a moment. "But why would he spare Rodney and not Dexter? Does God have favorites? Does he have only a limited amount of miracles to go around?"

"An old priest once told me that after all the years he had spent serving the Lord, he knew for certain only two things."

"Which are?"

"One, that there is a God, and two, that *he* wasn't him. Mike, I wish more than anything that at this moment I could give you a one-size-fits-all answer to all of your queries, but I can't. I don't know the mind of God. No one does, and I refuse to speculate or allow doubt to compromise my faith by focusing on the things I don't know.

"Instead, I look to God's Word and his actions in the past. Have you ever read the story of Joseph in Genesis?"

Mike hunched his shoulders. "I guess . . ."

"God begins by sending Joseph a dream which foretells how one day his brothers will bow down to him in servitude. But immediately after the dream, Joseph is sold by his brothers into slavery and for many years is forced to endure all kinds of hardships. God was trying him through the fires of adversity, testing him to make certain that Joseph's faith would not falter, because it would someday be needed to save a nation.

"Unfortunately, man looks only to tomorrow, but God looks over eternity and sees how our sufferings will someday benefit mankind. We must always remember, our primary purpose here on earth is to serve God through serving others."

"But what good could come out of our family's tragedy?" Mike asked.

"I don't know, Mike," Father James answered. "But this I do know, that God can and will turn everything to good if we just trust him."

"How can any possible good come out of this?"

"You're trying to *think* this through, Mike, instead of *trusting* it through." Father James leaned in closer. "God doesn't ask us to reason, he asks us to trust. Our finite minds cannot grasp the complexities of God's plans, plans that are infinitely greater than anything we could ever imagine."

Mike sighed. "Lorraine is convinced that God is going to re-store our son, but what if that doesn't happen?"

"Then God will give you the grace to bear it."

"I don't know if I can," he cried.

Father James sat quietly until Mike's tears had been spent; then, reaching for the Bible that lay on the counter, he asked, "How much do you know about heaven?"

Chapter Eight

❧❧

Mrs. *Norris* hastily scribbled a note.

Dear Father James:
Had to take Ethel to see about her car. Lunch is in the fridge. Chicken salad with walnuts and apples and a touch of dill. Just the way you like it, so don't say I never make you anything special. The cherry cheesecake is for the quilters' meeting tomorrow, so don't touch it. Didn't have time to make another dessert, so have an apple. You could use the fiber. Back in a few hours.

Mrs. Norris

She hurried next door to her house and opened the garage door, thinking she had about four hours to run Ethel over to Tri Town Auto and do a few errands before she had to be back for Rodney. His father would pick him up after dinner when he returned home from the hospital.

She carefully backed her Subaru Outback out of the driveway and headed down the street. Sister Bernadette was raking leaves, while Father Keene stood at the ready with a wheelbarrow. She honked the horn. They waved.

She turned onto Main Street, passing by the familiar storefronts, and noticed that Secondhand Rose was having a two-for-one spring special. That reminded her. She'd better clean out Father James's closet and start sorting out his summer things. She seemed to remember that he was in need of some new short-sleeve shirts. The ones he had worn last summer were looking rather threadbare. Father James didn't care a fig about clothes. Last year the judge and Marge Peale had brought him home a beautiful cable-knit sweater from their trip to Ireland, and what did he do with it? He gave it away to one of the men at the homeless shelter.

But then, Father Dennis wasn't much better. Most of his clothing looked as though it were used for baby bibs. The man just couldn't seem to get the hang of using a napkin properly.

She rolled down the car windows and a light breeze, as soft as a whisper, tipped in hyacinths, sweetened the air. She felt a new song in her heart, an almost irresistible urge to keep on driving up and down the countryside, drinking in the landscapes dressed in spring down, reveling in the birdsong that filled the valley. This winter had been far too long.

As she turned onto School Street, she was greeted by children's happy squeals. The children outside the elementary school were engaged in a spirited game of soccer; their winter coats were thrown all about a small knoll in a patchwork design.

At this moment she longed to be a child again and recapture the wonder of the first day of spring filled with a sense of freedom and adventure. What new things were waiting to be discovered now that their world had awakened from its winter slumber?

She had a rich cache of memories from growing up in Dorsetville, among them that first day of spring, which always seemed to appear on a school day. How hard it was to concentrate on times tables and the conjugation of verbs as the season's seductive refrains echoed outside the windowpanes.

The school day would seem interminable, but finally the last buzzer would sound, and they would spill out of the building and rush over newly plowed fields, at moments feeling as though they could fly. Coats, hats, and gloves were left in their wake, causing parents great concern the next morning when winter tried to briefly reassert itself.

Next went the shoes and socks as they trudged down to the low swamps to feel the thick, cool mud curl around their toes. Then down to the lake, making bets as they went along. Would the rope they used to swing out over the cerulean blue waters last summer still be there? It usually was, and almost always someone would test it and "accidentally" fall in.

Mrs. Norris slowed to a crawl, passing the front of the school. It hadn't changed much since she had gone to school there. Rodney was in one of those classrooms right now, but she doubted that he was thinking of spring.

Today was his first day back since the accident. Mike had dropped him off at her house this morning on his way to the hospital. The sight of the poor child had nearly broken her heart. Never had she seen a child look so forlorn. She wished there was something that she could have said to help him weather this storm. It was going to be tough going back to school alone.

She had watched him walk out to the sidewalk, bent like a shoe hook. It looked as though the backpack he had slung over his shoulder must weigh a ton, but of course, that just wasn't so. She had packed it with his lunch, lifted it herself. It hadn't weighed more than a few pounds. No, it wasn't the weight of what was in that pack that was weighing him down. It was what was on his heart, where he carried the loss of both a brother and a best friend.

She took a shortcut that wound its way toward the north side of town and toward Ethel's house, her thoughts still on Rodney.

Who is Jennie? he had wanted to know.

As far as she knew, the Gallaghers hadn't known she had had a daughter.

What exactly had he said?

I heard Dexter's voice that night after the accident. He said I was to tell you that Jennie was there and that she had come to show him the way. Who is Jennie?

Could Jennie have actually come to help Dexter cross over to heaven?

Honey followed her mistress inside Tri Town Auto's office, happy to be free at last from the confines of Mrs. Norris's compact car with the freshly laundered sheet that smelled of bleach laid across her backseat.

Their car was in for repairs, along with the blanket that Honey favored, which smelled of dog biscuits, flea powder, and Mrs. Stilton's henhouse, which they frequented often for eggs.

Nancy Hawkins looked up briefly from a sheaf of paperwork and gave Ethel a wan smile. She and her husband, Don, were the owners of Tri Town Auto, which at the moment was several days behind schedule.

Right now, John Moran's Toyota 4Runner was suspended in midair, showcased in the plate-glass window behind the service counter. The sharp staccato blast of an air gun filtered through. Don dropped a wrench and swore. Honey whined softly and leaned heavily against Ethel's leg.

"She doesn't like loud noises," Ethel explained, rubbing the dog between the ears.

"Can't say as I blame her," Nancy said, hunched over a thick pile of work orders in search of her appointment book. "It'll be a miracle if I'm not stone deaf by the time I'm fifty."

"You do look awfully busy," Ethel said, trying to find a tactful way to ask when her car would be ready. It had been in the shop since Monday.

"We've had three tow-ins this morning. Sheriff Bromley's Blazer blew a head gasket, which needs to be fixed right away, and we still haven't caught up with last week's workload." She rubbed her forehead. "If only I could get rid of this headache. I've had it for days."

"It must be all the stress you're under," Ethel offered.

"You're probably right. That plus a lack of sleep. Don and I were here until eleven last night. I'm dead on my feet. But enough about my troubles. Now, when was your car due to be picked up?"

She pulled her tattered, grease-stained appointment book out of the rubble.

"Dear Lord . . . I'm further behind than I thought. Says here that your car was scheduled for Tuesday, and it's already Friday. Friday? It can't be Friday yet, can it? Where did the rest of the week go?"

Nancy looked past Ethel and out into the parking lot, where a dozen more automobiles were lined up waiting to be repaired, and sighed. "I'm so sorry, Ethel. I'm beginning to lose hope of ever catching up."

"Will it be much longer?"

"If I can hold off on Chester Platt's value job, maybe a week."

"That long?" Her face fell.

The phone rang. Nancy let the machine pick up. "If only we could find another mechanic. We've been advertising for months now. We get a lot of high school kids who want to apply, but no one with the kind of experience we're looking for."

The connecting door to the office creaked open and Nancy's husband, Don, came in searching for a repair order.

"I put it behind the front visor like always," she told him.

"It's not there. I looked," he said, chomping down on his cigar.

"Then look again."

"You need a better system."

"The system is fine," Nancy said with a slight edge to her voice.

"Well, it ain't working now," Don growled.

The husband and wife team had worked together amicably since high school, but lately increased business pressures had started to take their toll. Most nights they barely spoke to each other on the ride home.

"Then *you* find a system!" She slammed the appointment book on the counter.

"I'm tired of taking the blame for everything that goes wrong around here," Nancy said hotly.

Honey jumped to her feet.

The phone rang again, adding to the clamor.

"Aren't you going to answer that?" Don asked his wife.

"You answer it."

"You're standing right next to it. Why don't—"

"I have a good mind just to walk out of here and let you handle the paperwork," Nancy challenged.

Ethel slipped quietly out the front door. She'd try again next week.

"I don't know why they're having so much trouble finding a mechanic. It's not like they're looking for a brain surgeon," Mrs. Norris said, driving past the old Stilton place. "You need eggs?"

"No, I picked some up last week."

"I hope she finds one soon. My car is due for an oil change."

"If I were you, I'd think about taking it to Lucky Lube."

"I don't trust those people. Did you hear about Mary Pickett?"

Ethel told her she hadn't.

"She took her Ford Explorer over there for a simple oil change. Twenty minutes later, one of those young kids walks into the waiting area and shows her a dipstick oozing with this vile black stuff and proceeds to tell her that both her transmission fluid and break fluids are badly in need of changing. If she doesn't get it done now, he says, it will clog up her engine, causing costly repairs. She figures that he must know what he's talking about, so she gives him the go-ahead. Costs her thirty-nine ninety-five over the oil change, mind you.

"Well, next time she sees Nancy she tells her what Lucky Lube found and asks why Don let her car fluids go so long without being changed. And you know what Nancy says? She said they were changed a month ago. Imagine that. Those lying dogs. Nope, I'd rather wait for Nancy to get caught up."

"That might take a while," Ethel said sagely.

The day was so lovely that conversation wasn't necessary as they traversed along the back roads that gave way to broad vistas. It was a perfect day for taking a ride. Each woman was wrapped in her own secret thoughts, and for the next several miles they drove along in silence, until Mrs. Norris turned down an old dirt road that ringed a small lake about two miles outside of town.

Ethel turned to her with a smile. "Remember the summer we spent here as kids?"

"I sure do. Oh look, Ethel, I can't believe it. That old cabin is still standing. Well, I'll be darned. I would have thought that thing would have tumbled to the ground aeons ago."

"Pull over, Margaret. Let's take a look."

Mrs. Norris rolled onto the grass and cut the engine. The women leaned forward and stared out into the patch of woods that bordered the entrance to the lake.

"Remember the summer Kit O'Clary introduced us to Nancy Drew?"

"Oh my, I haven't thought about those books in years," Ethel said, laughing like a schoolgirl. What fond memories that evoked.

"I still have my collection, you know."

"Keep it. I hear it's worth a nice bit of change nowadays," Ethel offered.

"I couldn't sell them. I loved those books. You know, I wanted to be just like Nancy Drew."

"I think we all did," Ethel said, laughing.

"But how we loved them," Mrs. Norris remembered fondly.

"That we did," Ethel agreed.

And suddenly it was as if a breeze had caught the pages of a yellowed and aged scrapbook, whisking them back through time to the summer of 1952 and Nancy Drew.

Summers were a time for dreaming and the great outdoors when they were growing up. As soon as the buzzer rang on the last day of school, Margaret, Ethel, and Kit O'Clary would rush out the front door, pigtails flying behind them like kite tails, jump onto their bicycles, and ride into a summer that seemed never to end.

They were never bored or lacking adventures. There were always things to do and places to explore. In fact, summers were rich in adventures, and sometimes great mysteries—like exploring the history of the old cabin that sat in a thicket of woods about a mile or so down from the Stiltons' egg farm.

The wooden one-room cabin had been abandoned for nearly fifty years and was in peril of collapse. It sat on cinder blocks, the front steps having long ago been rotted out by termites. A wooden screen door hung from one hinge and banged in the wind, sounding like a repeater rifle. The sound had always sent them screaming into the woods as though the hounds of hell were on their tails.

The interior's one room was shrouded in spiderwebs, and its wooden floor had rotted out in sections, creating large black craters from which eerie sounds emanated. It smelled of moss and damp wood, for the windows had long ago been shot out in target practice by the neighborhood boys, who had since commandeered it as their secret clubhouse. And although it was primarily the boys' domain, the girls would often hunch down and creep through thick underbrush to peer inside.

By August, feelings of unrest would begin to stir like loose dirt on a country road. By now the boys had grown bored with imaginary games of war and Indian rebellions and sought more tangible conquests. The girls quickly became the enemy and the placid streets of Dorsetville echoed with terrified screams as the boys declared war.

But change came the summer of 1952 in the guise of small blue-covered books bearing the silhouetted shape of a slim girl bent over a magnifying glass. Her name was Nancy Drew, and Kit O'Clary discovered her first. Within the week, tales of Nancy's fearless escapades had spread among the gaggle of elementary school girls, changing their views on the role of women forever.

The novels depicted a girl who was fearless, who didn't sit by the sidelines but went out looking for adventure; and she found it.

She neither cooked nor sewed nor talked about marriage. She was her own woman and even the boy characters sat up and took notice when she was around.

Every one of the girls that summer wanted to be just like her.

The girls mowed through titles: *The Hidden Staircase, The Bungalow Mystery, The Haunted Bridge, The Clue of the Broken Locket, The Quest for the Missing Map*. Some were reading two or three titles a week.

Copies were shared and plots discussed, and by mid-August, passionate discussions were taking place while the girls sipped Kool-Aid beneath the tendrils of the weeping willow in Margaret Norris's front yard. In between, they'd play endless games of "What would Nancy do?"—which eventually brought them around to their own dilemma: how could they stop the boys from harassing them?

Kit was a natural leader and quickly decided that the first step should be a meeting with the boys.

For days, runners on both sides scurried back and forth between the two camps. Would their leader, Tommy White, meet alone with their leader, Kit O'Clary, or should all the boys and girls meet together? Since neither Tommy nor Kit relished the thought of being alone with the other, it was finally decided that both factions should meet as a group. There was safety in numbers.

Then there was the bigger issue—where would they meet?

The boys wanted to meet in the cabin. The girls preferred sunlight and meadows to dense forests and spiders and suggested under the willow tree, which brought waves of protests from the boys.

"Only sissies or *girls* sit under a tree."

For days notes flew back and forth. Location, as they say, is everything, and neither faction wanted to yield. The big meeting was in peril of never happening until the girls, in a moment of great magnanimity, decided that the cabin would be all right, after all.

Nigel Hayes, a runtlike boy in a striped polo shirt, sporting a cowlick the size of a horse's mane—his parents had just moved here from England, and his father taught English at the college across the river—had been elected to watch for the girls' arrival outside the cabin.

"They're here," he yelled, then produced a rusted tin bucket from underneath a row of mountain laurel. He pushed it up against the cabin's door.

"Step on this," he said impatiently with his crisp British accent, appearing anxious not to be separated from his peers any longer than absolutely necessary.

Twelve-year-old Tommy White sat in the middle of the floor—all 150 pounds of him, a roll of flesh stuffed like a large sausage link beneath his cotton pullover. He beckoned Kit to sit down on a scratchy woolen blanket that had been spread on the floor.

Several seconds of awkward silence followed. The boys stared up at the ceiling. The girls looked anxiously around for spiders.

Finally Tommy spoke. "So, what do you want?"

Kit's eyes zeroed in on Tommy's face, and in her best Nancy Drew voice she replied, "We want you to stop pestering us."

Tommy laughed out loud. "You want what?" Then he assumed an air of absolute innocence. "We're not bothering you."

"Ha!" Kit laughed with contempt.

The girls recognized that laugh. Nancy laughed that way whenever her sidekick Ned tried to dismiss her superior analytical mind.

"What do you call water balloons crashing down on our heads from the treetops, or garden snakes slithering out of our mailboxes?" she asked.

Tommy snickered. "What's the matter? Can't you take a little joke?" He turned to his buddies. "Girls are such sissies."

The boys laughed nervously.

"We are *not* sissies," Kit stated emphatically. "We've had enough, and we want it to stop!"

"Well maybe we will and maybe we won't." Tommy folded his arms across his chest.

"What are they going to do if we don't?" one of the boys asked.

"Yeah," the others chimed in.

Unfortunately, the boys never sensed the danger. Blinded by testosterone, they never saw the challenge. What boy would ever seriously consider a girl a threat? Why, that was laughable! As far as Tommy White was concerned, Kit O'Clary was the same blond-haired, ponytailed girl that he had known and teased all of his life, who had always gone home crying to her mommy.

But that was BND (before Nancy Drew). Tommy was about to be blindsided. He didn't recognize the metamorphosis that had taken place.

"If you tease us one more time or play one more prank, I will punch you right in your fat face," Kit threatened. The gauntlet had been thrown.

The girls gasped at the blatant audacity of the statement.

The boys were stunned into silence.

It took Tommy several seconds to recover, then he scrambled to his feet, hands on hips. He towered over Kit like a colossus.

"You scare me. You *really* scare me, Kit O'Clary. See, I'm shaking in my shoes."

Kit later said that she had felt a certain detachment looking up at the silver fillings that lined Tommy's mouth. She slowly rose to her feet and stood eyeball to eyeball with the bully who had stolen so many golden, sweet moments of summer.

She felt his hot, putrid breath against her face. Saw the mockery in his eyes. It was at that moment that Kit O'Clary knew that she must make a decision. Not just for her, but for all girls who had ever been bullied by boys. Was she going to back away and run or, worse, cry? Or would she strike out for girls everywhere?

What happened next became legend around Dorsetville and was still occasionally remembered at certain social functions.

That day Kit O'Clary punched Tommy White right in the face and broke his nose.

Honey began to whine from the backseat. Ethel's house was just up around the bend.

"I wonder whatever happened to Kit O'Clary after she moved that next year," Mrs. Norris mused, turning into Ethel's driveway. "Did you ever hear from her again?"

Ethel and Kit had once been the best of friends. "No."

"You and she had a falling-out right before she moved away. What happened?"

"It was a foolish, childish thing, really," Ethel said, gathering her purse. "One day I happened to walk past the cabin and discovered Kit and Tommy White kissing. Somehow it felt like the ultimate betrayal."

Chapter Nine

❦❧

*D*r. *Iannini,* the chief of neurology at Mercy Hospital, was short in stature and short on patience, but considering the circumstances, he was working hard to maintain a professional calm. Dexter Gallagher had lain in a coma for over a week and by all indications would not recover from his injuries, and the doctor felt that it was time for the family to approve the removal of the respirator and get on with their lives.

He was fairly certain he could persuade the father, but the mother remained adamantly opposed. Complicating the issue was the family priest, a Father James, who sided with the wife and who, at this moment, was trying to make a point.

"I've read of other patients who have been in comas for far

longer than Dexter and have finally come out of it. Why not wait?"

How many times had they been over this, a dozen? Dr. Iannini thought. He reined in his impatience and tried to explain one more time.

"Because it would be cruel to do so," he said, removing his glasses and slipping them inside the lab coat pocket. "The cases you've mentioned were entirely different from this. All of them registered some level of brain activity. Dexter does not." He turned to plead with the Gallaghers. "I know that this is hard on you both. He's such a young boy. But the indisputable fact remains that the son you knew is no longer with us, and he will not return."

"Don't say that!" Lorraine shouted, rising from her chair beside Dexter's bed.

"It's all right," Father James said, placing a restraining hand on her shoulder.

"Whether you want to hear it or not, Mrs. Gallagher, your son *is* gone," Dr. Iannini said, with a clinical edge to his voice. "These machines are the only things that are keeping him alive."

"Good morning," said Doc Hammon's replacement, who had just stepped into the room. "I thought you two might need some support."

Father James sighed with relief. He had met Dr. Noiyst earlier and had taken an instant liking to this personable young man. Maybe he could convince the neurologist to give Dexter more time.

"We're so glad to see you," Lorraine said, hope returning to her eyes. She had been devastated over Doc Hammon's absence, but his replacement had proven every bit as compassionate and kind. She trusted him implicitly and felt an enormous release of tension now that he had arrived.

"I'm Dr. Nathan Noiyst," he told the neurologist. Then, looking down at the slumbering child, he asked, "So how's our patient today?"

"That's just what I've been trying to explain to the Gallaghers." Iannini handed him the boy's chart. "As you can see, there's been no change. It's time to take him off the respirator."

Dr. Noiyst flipped through the sheaf of papers. Finally he closed the folder and handed it back. "Why don't we give the boy another week?"

"What will that accomplish?"

"It would give this couple time to prepare for what you say is inevitable, and seven more days for God to provide the miracle they're seeking."

Dr. Iannini elected to ignore the part about God or possible miracles. "You're a medical doctor. The facts are right there on that chart. The boy will not regain consciousness based on what we have observed, and the medical tests prove me out."

"Yes, I would agree that they're not very encouraging, but there is more to the child lying in that bed than what's indicated on that chart."

He walked over and took Dexter's hand in his. "Inside this small body lies a divine spark, a spirit, and until I am totally convinced that that spirit is gone, I cannot agree with your assessment," he challenged.

Father James felt a sudden energy charge through the room, displacing the dark pall with the bright light of hope. He hoped Doc would consider keeping Noiyst on when he returned.

Dr. Iannini studied the young physician as though trying to decide whether to push his point or concede. Finally he decided that since Dr. Noiyst was the child's primary physician, it would help matters if he were to have his consent when he went forth with the legal proceedings.

"All right. I'll give you one more week. But after that, whether you agree or not will be irrelevant. This hospital will seek a court order to remove all life supports."

It had been a quiet morning at dispatch for Betty Olsen. The sheriff was in a meeting with the mayor and only one call had come in all morning. Mildred Dunlop had reported a garbage can rolling down the road outside her house. Betty dispatched one of the deputies in the cruiser to take care of it.

Later, her sister-in-law Shirley called to say that Doc Hammon had just been wheeled into surgery, and asked her to increase her prayers. And since things were slow at the moment on both sides of the phone, they went on to talk about Dr. Noiyst, whom all the patients seemed to love, and Doc's poor eating habits, which both felt had landed him in this sorry mess.

"You'd think that as a doctor, he'd know better," Shirley said, accompanied by the rustle of papers. She was getting ready to send off some insurance claims. "I don't ever remember seeing that man eat a vegetable."

The topic of food reminded Betty that she had wanted to try that new low-carb diet Shirley had raved about. Shirley had lost ten pounds in two weeks and had gained back her curves. Shirley promised to fax it right over as soon as they hung up.

Seconds later, the dispatch phone rang.

"Dorsetville Police Department. Please state your emergency," Betty said.

"Hi, Betty. This is Principal Kemple over at the elementary school. We seem to be missing a student this morning."

"Who?"

"Rodney Gallagher. It's his first day back since . . . well . . . you know. His class was scheduled for music appreciation this period, but when the teacher took roll call, he was missing. We've searched everywhere—the building, the grounds—but he's nowhere to be found.

"I don't want to trouble his parents if it can be avoided, so I was wondering if you could send one of your deputies to have a look around town. He couldn't have gotten far."

Deputy Hill turned up the collar of his heavy woolen jacket and headed out. If the boy was anywhere in town, he'd find him. He'd leave no stone unturned.

Poor kid, Hill thought. He'd heard Dexter wasn't doing well.

The thought triggered another, and he took out a small pocket calendar that he had purchased earlier that morning at the smoke shop. Using his front teeth to pull off his right-hand glove, he took out a pencil and under the slot allotted for March 25, he wrote, *Visit Saint Cecilia's. Light a candle.* He figured that since things had worked out so well after soliciting Saint Anthony's help on his own behalf, maybe the saint could help out in finding the boy.

He calculated the amount of time needed for this errand of mercy and figured it would take him ten, maybe fifteen minutes to visit the church, light a candle, and say a few prayers. He blocked out an appropriate time slot right after lunch, then slipped the calendar back inside his coat pocket.

Keeping track of every minute spent throughout the day was another golden principle stressed by the Tapping the Power Within program. According to Rich Malone, time was the currency of the universe.

"Successful men and women make every minute count," he counseled. "Learn to carefully plan your day."

Hill was scrupulously adhering to the program and was pleased as a horse in clover at how things were working out. During the first segment, he had learned the power of visualization.

"Form follows thought," Malone preached.

It had taken him a few days to get the hang of it, but eventually he could actually see the sheriff inviting him into his office to deliver the news that Hill had been put back on days. Much to his amazement, that's exactly what happened a few days later. Hot dog!

Hill was blissfully ignorant, however, of the new union contract that had just been put into effect, which required the sheriff to pay time and a half to anyone who patrolled after eight o'clock at night. Instead, he saw the shift change as just another confirmation that his self-improvement course was working.

Now as he walked down Main Street in search of Rodney Gallagher, he adjusted his earphones and hit the cassette's Play button.

"Problems are simply seeds for the soul's advancement . . ."

"Problems are the seeds for the soul's advancement," he intoned. "Problems are the—"

Wait a minute! It suddenly hit him like a thunderbolt. This wasn't about finding a missing boy. The universe had deliberately arranged for Rodney to be missing, so he could hone his detective skills. Wasn't that one of his chief goals? Ten years from now he planned to have risen through the ranks to detective.

The thought spun him around like a turntable.

Images ran through his head like a Hollywood movie. It opened on a crime scene. A million dollars' worth of diamonds had just been stolen from a New York penthouse. Enter Hill, the lead character, dressed in an expensive Italian suit, the jacket tailored to hide his Smith & Wesson. As he entered the room, rookies parted like the Red Sea.

"Make way," someone said, with a touch of awe in his voice. "Detective Hill has arrived. Now the case will be solved."

The reverie ended when a catfight broke out in one of the alleyways. Seconds later, his walkie-talkie crackled with Betty's voice.

"Hill, I just got off the phone with Marge Peale. She saw Rodney about twenty minutes ago heading across the Grand Union parking lot."

"Roger. I copy. Tell everyone to rest easy. Detective . . . er . . . Deputy Frank Hill is on the case."

From the backseat of Sam's Plymouth, Rodney watched Deputy Hill disappear inside the Country Kettle. The thought of one of Harry's cheeseburgers and a chocolate malt sure made him hungry. He hadn't eaten since early this morning. If he had stayed in school, it would have been lunchtime by now. Today they were serving chicken fingers, one of his favorites.

The wind was blowing something fierce outside. Rodney had nearly frozen his face off on the walk down from the schoolyard. Just his luck. Yesterday it was as warm as spring. Today the arctic chill had returned. At least the car offered him a warm haven and a place to think things out. He hadn't thought much further than escaping school. Now what should he do?

The temperature was rapidly dropping inside the car and the cold was seeping in through his nylon parka. His teeth began to chatter. He couldn't stay here much longer. He'd freeze to death. But where would he go? One thing was for certain, he was never going back to school again. Not ever.

A hot tear settled in the corner of his eye. Rodney shoved it away with an angry hand. He remembered Dexter's empty chair. It wasn't like the times it was empty because his brother had the flu or when he'd gotten his nose broken with a hockey stick. This was how it might be forever if Dexter died. Suddenly he felt an emptiness inside him. What would he do without his brother, his best friend? Nothing would ever be the same without him.

He felt a deep sadness tighten across his chest and he knew he was about to cry. Before he could break down like a blabbering baby, he diverted his attention outside. People were scurrying along the sidewalk like sails under a strong wind.

What was he going to do? He couldn't stay here all day. He wished Dexter were here. He'd think of something. The tears returned.

"Sure you don't need a ride over to the television station?" he heard Mr. Rosenberg say. Rodney hid on the floor.

"Thanks, but we have more shots to film over at the library," Ben said, balancing the camera case. Since finding the anonymous note in Sam's car, he had decided never to leave the camera unattended. "Then we have to meet with the mayor. He's going explain the new budget cuts on this week's show."

"How will you get back?"

"Matthew is picking us up when he gets out of school. Then he'll hang around at the station and help edit what we've shot." Ben's teenage grandson was a whiz at the technical stuff that completely mystified the older men.

"I thought you had someone down at the station that did that," said Sam, walking around to the driver's side of his car.

"We did," Timothy explained. Today he was dressed in a sheepskin coat that was several sizes too large and tied with a rope.

Sam tried not to stare. "So what happened?"

"He quit. Got a better offer at a news station over in Hartford."

"I just hope that we can continue to rely on Matthew," Timothy said, pulling on a knit cap.

"Why shouldn't we?" Ben asked, defensively. After all, this was his grandson they were talking about, not some teenage kid they had pulled off the street.

"Girls," Timothy said sagely.

"Oh, yeah," Ben said soberly. He had forgotten about the girls.

Sam pulled into the senior center's parking lot and headed inside. It was a low brick building built in the fifties, when floor-to-ceiling windows, lots of chrome, and the color aqua were in vogue.

The director, Mrs. Hopkins, was in her office, seated behind a desk talking on the phone. Sam caught her eye and she motioned him to come in.

Cupping the phone with her hand, she said, "You have a new client. Mrs. Hudson over on Meadow Street. She's broken an arm, so she'll need meals delivered until the cast comes off."

She handed him a form completed in her perfect longhand.

"I'll take care of it," Sam said, pausing briefly to riffle through the ceramic bowl filled with Hershey's candies she kept on her desk. He chose one with almonds, then headed off toward the kitchen.

Since it was nearing noontime, the kitchen was a hub of activity. Prepackaged dinners were being heated in the warming ovens; one woman was cutting up a sheet cake into two-inch squares; another was setting up the coffee urn. Someone else was packing the hot dinners into insulated containers. As soon as he stepped through the doorway, a chorus of "Hi, Sam" resounded.

"Good morning, Samuel," Mary Krause said as he neared her workstation. She was in charge of boxing the lunches.

Almost everyone except Sam knew that Mary had a secret crush on him. She also knew that his loyalties lay with Harriet Bedford, but this didn't stop her from hoping.

"I have everything ready," she said, pointing to the two-tiered metal cart stacked with meals.

"What's on today's menu?"

"Creamed beef on toast points, roasted new potatoes, string beans, and a piece of white cake with orange icing. I packed an extra piece of cake. I put it right there on the top. I thought you might like some later with a cup of tea," she said, blushing.

Sam thanked her and headed out toward the parking lot with the cart, down the handicap ramp, and around the two large potholes that had emerged over the winter. He opened the trunk of his car and expertly packed the containers inside, then stuffed woolen blankets he kept just for this purpose around the edges, shoring them up. When he was certain that all was secure, he slammed the trunk lid down hard and double-checked that it was properly fastened. The one time he had forgotten to check, he had hit a bump and the release unlocked, sending River Street clients' dinners sailing all over the countryside.

Sam was mulling over the best way to incorporate Mrs. Hudson into his route, and not paying much attention to anything else, when he opened the Plymouth's back door and Rodney Gallagher popped out like a jack-in-the-box.

"Hello, Mr. Rosenberg," the boy said. Thinking quickly, he added, "I thought you might need some help delivering your meals."

"How is he?" Shirley asked Joan Hammon.

Doc had been operated on this morning and she had been on pins and needles, waiting for his wife to call.

"He's fine, Shirley," Joan told her with a tired edge to her voice. "I spoke with his doctor and he said that Jack came through the operation with flying colors. But as you know, the next twenty-four hours will be critical. We're not out of the woods yet."

"You tell that big lug to hang in there," Shirley said, fumbling for a tissue. "And remind him that we're all praying for a quick recovery. Dr. Noiyst is a lovely man and wonderful physician, but no one can really replace our Doc."

"Thank everyone for their prayers. The thought of anything happening to him . . ." Joan began to break down.

"Nothing's going to happen to him," Shirley said with an authority that surprised even her. "We just won't let it."

Betty hung up the phone after speaking with Sam and buzzed Hill on his walkie-talkie.

"Sam Rosenberg just called," she told him. "Rodney was hiding out in the backseat of his car. He's dropping him back at school on his way out to deliver meals. No, I don't think you have to do a follow-up investigation. No, I don't think you should suggest to Principal Kemple they need to put surveillance cameras up around the school.

"Sorry, but I didn't hear that last part. The sheriff just stormed in looking fit to be tied. He and the mayor must have had another fight over budget cuts.

"Why don't you stop over at the Country Kettle and get him a roast beef sandwich on a hard roll? That should cheer him up. Extra mayo, and get me one, too. And an order of fries. Oh . . . and tell Lori to put in one of her éclairs. Make it two."

After looking over the low-carb diet Shirley had just faxed over, Betty decided to wait a while before giving it a try.

Chapter Ten

"Over here,"** Harriet called as Sam entered the Country Kettle.

She and Ethel were settled in a booth, warming themselves over mugs of coffee by the side window that looked out onto the entrance of Linden's Funeral Home. Marge Peale had dropped them off after quilting.

"We were getting worried," Harriet told Sam, watching him unwind the woolen scarf she had knitted him for Hanukkah last year. "I thought you were meeting us right after you delivered your meals."

"I had another drop-off to make," he chuckled, sliding in beside her. "Rodney Gallagher tried to stow away in my car."

"He what?" Harriet exclaimed.

The women leaned in as Sam related how he had found the

young boy in the backseat. "I'm afraid that he's lost without his brother."

"That poor child," Harriet said. "It makes me feel so awful for all the times I wanted to wring their necks. So, where is he now?"

"I dropped him back over at the school. I told Mr. Kemple that if there was anything I could do to help, to let me know."

Wendy paused en route to another table. "I see you've finally made it, Sam. The women are having a bowl of soup. You want one? It's beef barley today."

"Sounds good to me," Sam said.

"Sam, I hate to impose," Ethel began, "but I was wondering. Could you drop me off at Tri Town after lunch? My car is supposed to be ready this afternoon."

"No trouble at all," Sam said, studying the menu although he knew it by heart. "Harriet and I are headed out that way. We're going to Kmart."

"I have to pick up another skein of yarn to finish that scarf I'm knitting for the church raffle," Harriet explained, breaking off another piece of buttered roll and plopping it into her mouth. She hadn't had a bit to eat since six o'clock this morning and she was starved.

"What church raffle?" Ethel asked.

"Oh, that's right. You weren't at the Altar Guild's last meeting. We've decided to host a raffle to help pay some of the Gallaghers' hospital costs, so if you have anything you'd like to donate . . ."

"Count me in. I'm sure I can come up with something."

Sam watched Harriet polish off another roll and suddenly felt like a sandwich. He scanned the day's specials but couldn't find any mention of his favorite, corned beef. He flagged Wendy down as she flew past again.

"I thought Harry served corned beef sandwiches on Tuesdays."

"He does," Wendy said.

"And . . . ?"

"Today is Wednesday."

"Oh. Then I'll have just the soup," he said, wondering how he had managed to misplace a whole day.

Wendy cleared away the last of the mismatched luncheon plates, cups, and silverware. Although she had been here since early this morning, her uniform and white apron were spotless. And why not? After all, she was a professional waitress.

Wendy took enormous pride in her work, and she felt others should do the same. It didn't matter if you dug ditches for a living or worked in a high-tech lab searching for a cure for cancer. As far as she was concerned, all work was honorable and should be treated as such. If there was one thing she couldn't tolerate, it was people who acted as though one job were loftier than another. It ran counter to her philosophy that God gave each of us a talent with which to better serve mankind. To downgrade that gift was to spit in God's face.

Wendy loved what she did. She loved its diversity (no two days were ever the same), its fast pace (time never dragged), and the freedom it afforded. In between the customers and the kitchen, she was her own boss.

She arrived each morning at 5:45 on the dot, and set right to work. Mornings at the Country Kettle could get busier than Times Square on New Year's Eve. First she set up the coffeepots, since Harry's customers could down enough coffee in one morning to fill a small tanker. Next, she set out racks of cups and saucers. Then she set out ketchup bottles, sugar bowls, jelly holders, creamers, butter dishes, and salt and pepper shakers, making certain that each was filled to the brim.

By six-fifteen everything would be in place, ready for the first customers, who started piling in by six-thirty, even though Harry didn't officially open until seven. And by seven-fifteen, the place was packed.

Wendy had quit school when she was sixteen, after years of struggling through her studies. Later, she would be diagnosed as dyslexic, but back then they simply labeled kids like her "slow." She had hated that term, with its implication that she was stupid. She knew better. So she left on the day of her sixteenth birthday and never looked back.

She landed her first job as a waitress at a diner called On Parade, in Queens. It was frequented by construction workers in the morning, junior executives in the afternoon, and families in the evening. The pace was frantic; the owners were hotheaded Greeks who had little patience for customers who sent back food or for waitresses who messed up orders, but she loved it.

When her niece Harvest had finished high school, Wendy had thought that perhaps she might try waitressing. Like her aunt, Harvest had never been a good student. But Harvest surprised everyone by taking a job as an auto mechanic, and found she was quite good at it. She had the patience many men lacked, which gave her the edge in diagnosing tricky mechanical problems.

Eventually Harvest's talents were noticed by a young man by the name of Greg Forrester, who specialized in professional racing cars. The two teamed up and she was soon traveling around the country on the race-car circuit. Wendy could always spy her postcards in the stack of mail. They were the ones with the grease-stained edges.

Within a year, Greg and Harvest had fallen in love and were

married. The postcards continued to come, now filled with talk of the couple's dream of opening their own garage and their plans to purchase a tumbledown colonial they were going to fix up, then fill to the rafters with kids. What wonderful dreams they had then. And now . . .

A cloud covered the sun, and she felt a momentary sense of sadness. She grabbed a brown plastic tray from underneath the front counter. There was only one customer, seated in a small table by the kitchen door, who had been nursing the same cup of coffee since he'd come in, so she felt free to start cleaning up.

She began by removing the salt and pepper shakers off the tables. Every day they received a new slathering of grease and smudged fingerprints. She soaked a clean cloth in a pan of hot water and began to polish them, one by one. It was mindless work, but just the kind that would free her to puzzle out the issue concerning her niece.

Poor Harvest. Greg had been diagnosed with Lou Gehrig's disease. Harvest tried to care for him alone, but with his increasingly complex needs and her job, she had been forced to place him in a nursing home. A couple of weeks ago, she had sold the house they had so lovingly restored. The money was needed to pay for the mounting medical bills and nursing home fees.

Wendy finished polishing the shakers and started on giving the tables a thorough cleaning. She went about the task with an inordinate amount of force, scrubbing harder and harder the more she thought about her sister, Barbara's, indifference to Harvest's plight.

"I can't leave my job here in Orlando and move up north," Barbara had told her over the phone when Wendy called to tell her how desperate the situation had become.

"Then invite them to come down and stay with you," she said through clenched teeth.

"What? Here? You must be kidding. I couldn't bear it. You know that sick people make me nervous."

Wendy wanted to shake her, although she hadn't expected more. Barbara had always been incredibly self-centered.

Wendy and Harold talked it over and both agreed that Harvest should come live with them. She was arriving tonight.

Wendy glanced up at the clock. Maybe Harry would let her leave a little early today. Things were slow and she hadn't yet shopped for tonight's dinner. She wanted it to be something special. Maybe she'd call Gus and have him put aside a couple of strip steaks. Lord knows, the poor kid probably hadn't been able to afford one of those in a long time.

Wendy took a critical look around the restaurant. Everything was clean and tidy. She folded up her apron and went in search of Harry. Maybe she'd stop over at Tri Town on the way home. She had overheard the customers say that Nancy was looking for a mechanic. Harvest would need a job, and no one knew cars better than her niece.

"Hello, Mr. Rosenberg, this is Mr. Kemple from the elementary school. Rodney? Not good, which is why I'm calling.

"Remember how you said that if there was anything you could do to help the boy, I should give you a call? I wanted to know if your offer still stands.

"It does? Good, I thought it would.

"If you're free, I wonder if you wouldn't mind dropping over to the school later this afternoon. I have a proposal I'd like you to consider."

———

Arlene Campbell had just scheduled an appointment with Dr. Noiyst for Fred's blood workup. He was on several different kinds of medication, all of which had to be carefully monitored. Normally this wouldn't be a problem, but with Doc Hammon gone, she was concerned Fred might create a scene. He had grown increasingly wary of strangers. She wasn't at all certain what he might do when Dr. Noiyst tried to examine him. But whether Fred liked it or not, it had to be done. She just wished that it could be done with a little less angst.

She passed the hall mirror quickly, fearful of what it might reveal. Last time she looked, she had seen a tired, worn-out woman who had aged considerably over the last few months, with black circles underneath her eyes from lack of sleep, and in desperate need of a haircut.

Haircut? she thought. When was there time for a haircut? She could barely eke out enough time to eat. Caring for her husband had become a twenty-four-hour ordeal; there was precious little time left for herself. She was worn thin. How much longer could she go on being Fred's sole caregiver? She had tried an in-home caregiver, but Fred had become agitated. He didn't like strangers in his home. She had let her go. Now she was reduced to reliance on old friends. Thankfully, Fred still remembered who they were, but she dreaded the day when that portion of his mind also slipped beneath the inky depths of Alzheimer's.

Arlene was not a woman to wallow in self-pity, so she shook the doldrums and headed for her teakettle. She'd make herself a nice strong cup of tea. That would shake away the blues. It always did.

Father James had recently dropped off a container of the Harney & Sons peaches-and-ginger that she favored so highly. She snapped open the small black tin box and carefully scooped out a teaspoon of loose tea leaves, placing them into a small strainer that fitted snugly over the rim of a teacup.

She remembered fondly the last time she had visited their store in Salisbury, and the scent of myriad exotic teas from the farthest parts of the world that had greeted her as she stepped through. It was one of her favorite places to visit. She loved how she could choose from a variety of teas—Ceylon, China, Assam, Darjeeling, or one of the specially flavored black teas, like apple cinnamon, mango, black currant, citrus blend, and passion fruit—and one of the salesgirls would fix a cup to sample. She must have sampled most every one over the years.

The teakettle whistled and soon the kitchen was filled with the aroma of fruit and spices. She inhaled deeply, feeling fortified by this simple ritual. Perhaps its simplicity was what she relished the most. It provided stability in a world that had grown increasingly more complex.

She carried the china cup to the small wooden table beneath the kitchen window and collapsed into a chair. The television was playing softly in the living room, slightly masking Fred's rhythmic snores. In her mind's eye she could picture him stretched out on the sofa, his long legs dangling over the side. She used to love to see him sleep, the way the lines around his eyes would fade, hinting at the young man who had once come courting. Sadly, little of that man was now left to share those memories.

She sipped tea and wondered how much longer they could possibly go on like this. She was exhausted and just plain scared as Fred grew increasingly more difficult to care for each day. His sudden outbursts of anger frightened her the most. She had confided her fears to Doc before he left for surgery. He said it was to be expected as the disease progressed, and advised her to seek out a nursing home. She insisted that she could handle it, but now she wasn't so sure. Her arm bore black-and-blue marks from his last outburst of temper.

If only they had been able to have children. They would have helped to lighten the load. Children had been the only thing missing in their idyllic marriage. No two people had ever loved each other more dearly than she and Fred, which was why she was determined to hold true to her promise. Both had sworn that they would never place the other in a nursing home. She just prayed that she would find the fortitude to make good on that promise.

She suddenly realized that she had allowed her thoughts to focus on the hard times instead of the blessings they shared, like their many good friends.

Harriet called each morning.

"I can send Sam over if you need anything," she always offered, knowing that Sam would be happy to oblige.

And Ethel, bless her heart, came by twice a week to baby-sit Fred so Arlene could get caught up on the housework and laundry or—if Fred had had a fretful night—so she could take a nap.

There was Father James, a dear heart, always ready with a word of comfort. How many times over the last few months had she called the rectory in the depths of despair, only to hear his voice, gentle and kind, offering hope and encouragement? He also made certain to stop over once or twice a week to pay a call. She used these moments to fill up the well and looked forward to them like a woman in search of an oasis for her soul.

She watched a blue jay chase the chickadees off the bird feeder and rapped on the window to scare him away. The blue jay cocked one eye in her direction, surmised that she was not a threat, and stood his ground.

Perhaps she should adopt a similar stance, go about doing what she could for Fred and not let things weigh so heavily on her heart, especially thoughts for the future. But holding your mind steady and forging forward with hope was a lot easier on a full night's sleep, something that she hadn't enjoyed in over a week.

Fred had begun to wander around the house at all hours of the night. Last night he had gotten up to search for his childhood dog, Skip, and began to cry out in panic when Skip couldn't be found. She had tumbled out of bed and raced to see what was the matter, her chest constricting with fright. When she reminded him that Skip had been dead for nearly seventy years, he had become nearly inconsolable.

But it wasn't just her own well-being that she feared for. It was also Fred's safety. Twice he had gone outside unnoticed. Fortunately she had found him sitting on the porch swing, staring up at the sky. But what if he were to take off into the backwoods that bordered the town's land trust? There were two thousand acres of timber back there. It might be days before he was found, and in this harsh March weather, he could easily die. Her mind traveled back to the time Father Keene had wandered out into a blizzard. It was only through a miracle of God's grace that he found his way safely to Harriet's house.

The television channels in the other room changed in rapid succession. Fred had awakened. He paused on Regis and Kelly, his favorite morning show. For a short time, quiet would reign. Perhaps it would give her enough time to pack away her grandmother Hattie's china. She quickly drained her teacup, then took it over to the sink, rinsed it out, and set it on the counter before heading into the dining room.

Since moving into this house, the Royal Doulton china had adorned the dining room hutch. Friends had often admired this beloved heirloom down through the years. But yesterday Fred had tripped and nearly fallen into the cabinet. The pieces were filled with memories; and as much as she would miss seeing them line the painted shelves, she would be inconsolable should any get broken.

The clock above the kitchen sink read nine-thirty. Ethel had promised to be here at eleven. Poor dear, her car still hadn't been fixed, even though Nancy had sworn that it would be ready by late yesterday afternoon. Meanwhile, Sam was dropping her off on his way over to the senior center.

Should Arlene wait until they arrived, or dare to begin the project now? She had hoped to use Ethel's visit to catch up on her mending.

She peeked into the living room. Fred had moved over to the recliner and was napping again. At least someone was catching up on his sleep, she though wryly. She decided to take a chance. She had brought up some cardboard boxes from the barn yesterday and placed them on the back porch. She grabbed a handful of newspapers out of the recycling bin, stuffed them inside one of the boxes, and hurried back inside. The porch stood on the north side and was as cold as a tomb.

In contrast, the dining room was bathed in sunshine. She pulled aside the curtains and stared out into the sunlit day as though it were an aberration. She had grown so accustomed to the gray clouds that hung over the valley like a miasma, seeping through keyholes and under windowsills like the plagues once visited upon Egypt. Since their arrival, the Gallagher boy had fallen into the pond, Fred had grown increasingly worse, and Doc Hammon had been scheduled for surgery. She prayed the sunlight would stay.

She spread out several pieces of the *Dorsetville Gazette* on the dining room table, pausing briefly to scan the photos of the Gallagher twins on the front page. A fund-raiser was being planned by the Altar Guild on their behalf. She would have to search through her knitting basket and see what she might donate.

Once again, her heart filled with grief over this needless tragedy. Even though her life had been torn asunder since Fred's diagnosis, at least they both had lived a full and blessed life. Dexter had barely lived at all.

She set to work, carefully removing plates, bowls, cups, and saucers from the shelves and wrapping them in wads of newspaper. It was like holding memories in her hand. Fred's retirement dinner. Christmas Eve buffets before midnight mass. Summers spent on her grandmother Hattie's farm, with its gray goose, several Rhode Island reds, and fields of wildflowers.

Her father had been a college professor and geologist. He and her mother would roam the globe in search of new rock formations during summer semesters, while Arlene stayed behind on the farm. She never minded their absences. In fact, she much preferred the company of her grandmother, who taught her how to knit and crochet and how to roll pastry as thin as a piece of parchment.

But perhaps her fondest memory of those languid summer days was Sunday dinners. The house would be bursting with guests and the table adorned with her grandmother's best china.

"No use in saving it for a special occasion," she'd say. "Friends are special enough."

And special they must have been to eat off the Royal Doulton china, hand-painted by Grandmother Hattie's father, a master porcelain painter who had immigrated to America in the mid-nineteenth century.

"His pieces decorated some of the finest tables in Europe," Hattie would say with a great look of pride. Pointing to her father's mark, a fleur-de-lis, painted on the bottom of each piece, she would add, "There are collectors today that would pay a king's ransom for this set, but I would never part with it. Not for all the tea in China."

It was during the height of the Depression that that promise, however, was broken.

Arlene was ten years old and had once again come to stay with her grandmother. This time, however, her father was not traveling the world in search of rocks. Like millions of other Americans, he was traversing the back roads in search of a job.

One morning, Arlene came down to breakfast and noticed that the delicate teapot, creamer, and sugar bowl were missing.

"Grandmother," she called, alarmed, "someone has taken your china."

"No one has stolen it, dear. I've had to sell it," her grandmother explained.

"But you said that you wouldn't sell it for—"

"—all the tea in China, I know, child. But when I said that, I didn't have a grocer's bill that needed to be paid and no money to pay it with."

Arlene mulled this over. Knowing that her grandmother was a woman of great faith, she asked, "Why didn't you just tell God you needed the money?"

"I did."

"Then why didn't he give it to you, instead of having you sell your mother's china?"

Grandmother smiled and drew her close. "I don't know, child. But this I do know. The Lord has been my master, my teacher, and my best friend all of my life, and I trust him implicitly. I may not understand why he refused my request, but he has promised 'to turn all things to good.' "

"Even the sale of your mother's china?" she had asked incredulously.

"Even that."

Arlene had grown quiet, trying to take in this lesson of faith. Finally she said, "I wish that I could believe in God like you do, Nana."

Hattie kissed the top of her head. "Someday you will, but in the meantime, I'll hold you up with my prayers and believe for us both."

It was late morning when Arlene finished and headed toward the kitchen to begin on the breakfast dishes, which still lay in the sink. Never, in all the years since she had begun to keep house, had things ever been this untidy. She was just about to give in to feelings of guilt and shame when she remembered Father James's admonition the last time he had paid a visit.

On that day, Fred had insisted upon searching for an old baseball cap while Arlene was busy in the laundry room. She returned to discover that he had emptied every closet and bureau drawer onto the living room floor—and then the front doorbell rang. It was Father James, who had come to call. He found her on the verge of tears.

"You put Fred in for his nap. I'll straighten up in here," he told her.

"But Father, I can't . . ."

"Go." He gently swooshed her out of the room.

When she returned, Father James had shed his jacket and was busy folding a basketful of laundry.

"Oh Father, you shouldn't be doing that. Please sit down and let me get you a cup of tea. I'll take care of that later."

"Do you mind if I say something that's been on my mind for weeks?" he asked, folding one of Fred's undershirts.

"Why, no."

"Learn to ask for help. It's just as important to receive the help of others as it is to give. In fact, more so. Your needs become our opportunity to practice charity and compassion."

She tried to force a smile.

"It feels more like the practice of humility," she countered, placing a neatly folded tea towel on the pile designated for the kitchen drawer. "I've always taken great pride in maintaining a neat and orderly house, but just look at this place now. Stuff scattered all over the floor, dishes in the sink. I'm even ashamed to admit that I still haven't made up my bed."

He gave her a hug. "Don't worry. Your secret's safe with me."

Of course, Father James had been right, but still she found it difficult not to fight the urge to carry on as she had before Fred was taken ill. Wash and dusting on Monday; ironing on Wednesday; vacuuming and linens on Thursday; baking on Friday. At the beginning of Fred's illness she had been able to maintain this schedule, but as the disease grew worse, she found herself doing whatever she could whenever she could. Most things she just let ride. What was the use? Fred would only undo what she had cleaned or straightened in a matter of minutes. It was like living with a small child.

Bless Ethel and Harriet, who came often to help. Even Sister Claire visited once a week with a carload of nuns who made quick work of cleaning the house from top to bottom. And at times when things seemed especially dark and without hope, she would remember all these special kindnesses and try to give thanks.

Thanks for living in a small town where folks cared. Thanks for having a pastor whose prayers she often felt beneath her tired feet, raising her to new strengths. Thanks for the many good years she and Fred had shared together. Her only regret was that he no longer could share in the memories.

Sam's Plymouth pulled into the driveway. She glanced out the window and waved, then lifted the cardboard boxes off the table and carefully placed them safely out of harm's way.

"Hi, Arlene," Ethel called from the back of the house.

She hurried into the kitchen and was surprised to see Rodney Gallagher bounding through the door.

"Hello, Mrs. Campbell," Rodney said, with an armful of Ethel's supplies—knitting bag, tote bag, several shopping bags filled with baked goods. "Where do you want me to put these?"

"Over there on that chair," Arlene said. "Aren't you supposed to be in school?" She decided not to ask him about his brother.

"He's helping me," Sam offered, following behind with an armload of flowers. "And what about these?"

"Oh, Sam . . . they're beautiful."

He handed them over. "Harriet thought they might help lift your spirits."

Arlene buried her nose in the bouquet. "You tell her that they made them soar."

Sam laughed. "She'll love hearing that. Now, if you ladies don't need us anymore, we have some deliveries to make."

"Oh Sam?" Arlene said.

He turned.

"I hate to ask you for another favor, but—"

He silenced her. "Ask away."

What a dear, dear friend. "Fred needs some blood workup and I was hoping that you might—"

"What time's your appointment?" he asked.

"Four-fifteen."

"Then my sidekick and I will be here in time to get you there."

Both sets of Rodney's grandparents had died before he was born, so he was enjoying Mr. Rosenberg's company immensely. Unlike his parents, Mr. Rosenberg wasn't always telling him to do this or that; he really listened when Rodney spoke, and he didn't mind if Rodney ate Kraft macaroni and cheese for all three meals.

Rodney was glad that Father James had talked his parents into allowing him to stay with Mr. Rosenberg for a while. Father had also talked Mr. Kemple into letting Rodney do a study project about the Meals on Wheels program. That way he didn't have to go to class and answer the kids' stupid questions, like when was Dexter coming home and stuff like that.

Sam watched the boy out of the corner of his eye. Rodney's brow was furrowed in concentration. He was studying a town map. His teacher had suggested that Rodney hone his math skills by keeping track of their mileage and the distance between each point along their meal delivery route.

"It's three and a half miles to Mr. Hadley's place if we go up Painter's Ridge, but if we make a turn onto Maple and then onto Meadow Street, it's only three and a quarter miles," Rodney said, with some satisfaction at having been able to compute this. "It would save you some money in gas."

"Yeah? You sure?"

"Yes. I'm pretty good at math. Dexter is lousy. I always do his math homework."

Rodney set to work, bent over the yellow lined pad in his lap, but managed to keep one eye on the road, waiting for the turn up ahead.

"Turn up here," he instructed. "Then take the next left, and we should—"

Fenn's Pond came into view.

It was the first time Rodney had been here since the accident. Yellow police tape was still strung around the area. Wooden barriers with signs reading *Restricted Area—Keep Out* cordoned off a large section of the pond. Traces of tire tracks along the hillside made by the rescue equipment were still faintly visible.

Rodney stared out his side window for several moments, then slowly lowered his head and studied his nylon boots.

"He thinks it's my fault," Rodney whispered.

"Who does?" Sam asked.

"My father. He told my mother that I should have been watching Dexter and stopped him from skating so close to the edge."

"I'm sure he didn't mean it. He was probably just upset."

"That's what he said later, but I don't believe him."

No wonder the boy didn't want to go home, Sam thought.

"Your father must be very sad," he offered. "Sometimes we hurt so much that the only way we can survive the pain is to try and transfer it onto someone else."

Rodney thought for a moment. "It could have been my fault, you know. I should have watched out for Dex. He's kind of a klutz."

Sam smiled.

"I miss him. It doesn't seem the same without him." Rodney played with the cover to his ballpoint pen. "I can't remember ever not having him around. It's . . . it's going to be awful hard without him. Who's going to think up things to do? Dex always has great ideas," he finished rather proudly. Then he turned toward Sam and asked, "Do . . . do you think that Dex is going to get better?"

"Only God knows that, and I'm not God," he answered truthfully.

The two rode in silence. Finally Rodney asked, "Do you have any brothers or sisters, Mr. Rosenberg?"

"I did," he replied. "Both were killed in the Holocaust."

Rodney knew what the Holocaust was. He had studied it in school.

"How come you didn't get killed with them?"

"That, too, only God knows," Sam answered. "But since I did survive, I try to live each day as honorably as I can in their memory."

"Turn here, Mr. Rosenberg," Rodney said, pointing to a narrow driveway.

Sam pulled up the steep incline and parked alongside the back door.

"I think I will too," Rodney said quietly as Sam opened his car door.

"Think you will do what?"

"Live each day as honorably as I can in his memory. That is . . . if . . . Dex dies," Rodney said, with a catch in his throat.

Chapter Eleven

❦

"*It says here* that you're supposed to wait five seconds after the last frame before making a cut," Timothy told Ben. He was seated at the control booth at WKUZ, reading off a yellow sheet of lined paper that Ben's grandson, Matthew, had left. Matthew was supposed to be here, but he had just been grounded, which meant they would have to edit this week's *Around the Town* segment.

How hard could it be to splice some segments together? Ben had queried when they discovered they were on their own. Hadn't he and Timothy watched both the past editor and his grandson do it? It didn't seem hard. You just pushed this button and that, and there you were. Right?

To Timothy's left were several rows of neatly stacked tapes filmed over a period of several days in different locations. The plan was for Ben to splice marked segments together—Main Street, countryside shots—in the order that Matthew had laid out on the yellow pad.

But what had seemed so simple hours ago while Matthew explained it had grown increasingly more difficult and befuddling as the afternoon wore on. The fact that airtime was only a few hours away added to the mix, increasing the sense of impending doom, and soon the men, who had been best friends since childhood, were squabbling like kindergarteners.

"You're supposed to press the yellow button to import the next frames," Timothy instructed, his voice dripping with impatience. How many times did he have to say the same thing over and over?

"I *did* press the yellow button, but nothing happened. See?" Ben said, banging the yellow button with enough force to push it through the console.

"Well, you must be pushing the wrong button."

"There's only one yellow button," Ben said, his voice growing louder with each accusation. "How could it be wrong?"

"I don't know. You're messing up somehow," Timothy said, peering over Ben's shoulder.

"You want to move back a few paces, please. That shirt you're wearing is blinding me," Ben griped.

"And what's *wrong* with my shirt?" Timothy asked, poised for a fight.

"Nothing, come to think of it," Ben countered. "It goes with the rest of your outfit."

Timothy wore a luminous purple-and-orange striped knitted shirt with a torn pocket that he had duct-taped, and a pair of oversized green plaid trousers that he had tied with rope because he had misplaced his belt.

"Don't *ever* let Timothy in front of the cameras," Carl Pipson had once told Ben.

Ben fiddled with several dials that appeared to do nothing, then fell back into his chair in complete frustration.

"Darn thing. Here, give me that pad." Ben ripped the pad out of Timothy's hand. "Import? What the devil does 'import' mean?"

"I don't know, but we'd better find out soon. Airtime is at six P.M. sharp and it's already going on four o'clock."

"I know," Ben said testily.

"If only Matthew hadn't gotten grounded," Timothy lamented. "What was it this time?"

Ben tried to decipher Matthew's scribble. "Girls. Too much time talking on the phone and not enough studying. He got a C minus this quarter in calculus. Hand me that tape on the top of the pile, will you?"

"I knew girls would be our undoing. We should have hired another editor."

"We couldn't without Carl's okay."

"Then we should have called him."

"And ruined his vacation? I thought we wanted to prove that we were perfectly capable of handling things in his absence, or do you want to go back to being just two useless old men?"

"No. But do you really think we can pull this off? I mean, why don't we just run one of the old programs and blame it on technical failure?"

"We did that last week, remember?"

"Oh yeah. Someone sat on the tape and broke it."

"Someone?" Ben raised an eyebrow. Timothy had forgotten he had laid it on his chair when he went to answer the phone.

"Maybe we could chance another rerun. I mean, how's Carl going to know? He's on a ship somewhere in the middle of the Indian Ocean."

"You ever hear of something called e-mail?"

"Rats. I forgot about e-mail. Where the devil is a guy supposed to go to be alone these days?"

"Try the cemetery." Ben was back to fiddling with the dials. "Now, stop your jabbering and help me out here."

"I was helping out until you got all testy."

Ben glared.

"Okay, what do you want me to do?"

"See if you can get this dang thing to copy this segment onto the new cassette without destroying what we've already done, while I try and figure out how to dub the voice-overs."

For the next several minutes, both were absorbed in their tasks, each fighting against a rising sense of panic.

Ben tried not to look up at the clock. The production coordinator expected the finished tape an hour before airtime. That didn't give them much time.

Meanwhile, Timothy tried not to think about the friends who soon would be gathering at the Country Kettle to watch tonight's show. Who had started this Thursday night ritual, anyway? he wanted to know.

Harry kept the restaurant open past five o'clock so folks could watch the show and have dinner together. At a quarter to six, he would turn off the grill, lug the thirty-six-inch Panasonic out from his office, plop it down on the counter, and tune in to *Around the Town*. For the next sixty minutes, customers would be obliged to help themselves to drinks and desserts.

The studio clock ticked away the minutes, as Ben felt his

blood pressure rising and Timothy wondered if all of this aggravation was worth it. Why not fess up to not being equal to the task? So what if Carl might never ask them to serve as program managers again while he was away? Big deal! He could live with that, which, as far as Timothy was concerned, was far better than having a heart attack over this mess.

There was only one problem with this line of thinking. Ben would never go for it. It was a matter of pride, and heaven help anyone who got in the way of Ben's pride.

A light knock sounded on the control booth door.

"Mr. Metcalf, I'm so sorry to bother you," Gracie Abbott said, stepping lightly into the room. Gracie was WKUZ's receptionist and the most optimistic, upbeat person the town had ever known. Everyone loved her. Being next to Gracie was like bathing in sunshine.

The men waved her in.

"Your daughter-in-law Julie is on the phone. What a nice voice she has. I told her she should try out for that morning announcer position that's opening up next month. Well, anyway, Julie said she figured you'd be going to the Country Kettle afterward to watch your program. By the way, I just love the last two shows you men put together. I told my husband that most television footage puts ten years on you, but you men seem to have found the secret of taking off the years. Why, last week Mildred Dunlop looked five years younger."

Ben looked away. He figured there was no sense explaining that they were old episodes.

"Now, why did I come in here?" Gracie often lost her place and had to be "reprimed," as Carl called it.

"Julie called," Ben offered.

"Oh yes. She wants you to pick up some day-old challah

bread. She called Lori and she's holding it for you. Julie says it makes the best French toast she's ever tasted. Imagine, Lori knowing how to make challah bread. Is that a French bread, I wonder?"

"You can tell my daughter-in-law," he began, and paused. "Never mind, Gracie, I'll tell her myself."

"I don't mind delivering a message," Gracie said. "After all, it is my job."

A job she still fancied as the best job in the entire world. Where else could she meet *real* television personalities? It didn't matter to her if these personalities were plain local folk. Gracie looked upon most people with awe.

"That's all right, I want to ask my grandson something anyway." He pushed himself away from the editing console. "Maybe Matthew can explain what I'm doing wrong."

"Then I'll scoot ahead and I'll tell her you'll be right there." Gracie left humming the *Around the Town* theme song.

"I thought Matthew's phone privileges had been revoked," Timothy reminded him.

"I'm invoking grandfather privileges," Ben said, stepping out into the hall.

Timothy studied the rows of neatly stacked tapes that Matthew had arranged in sequential order. The yellow lined pad contained a listing of numbers, which correlated to the frames that needed to be copied onto the new tape.

"Run the tape and watch for the numbers to appear on the counter," Matthew had said, pointing to a small display window. "When you see the first number that coordinates with the number I've listed on the pad, push the Copy button. That will transfer the footage onto the new tape. Wait until you see the final number I've listed, then push Stop."

Matthew had made it seem so easy. Just line up the correct numbers taken off each tape, run the audio, and violà! You had tonight's segment.

But things were not going quite as smoothly as Matthew said they should. Timothy scanned the length of the console. He had seen Matthew edit tapes dozens of times. It hadn't seemed difficult. Ben had to be doing something wrong.

Normally, Timothy stayed clear of all this technical stuff. He was around to fetch and be Ben's backup. But what the heck? He might as well give it a try. They were goners if it wasn't completed in time anyway, so what difference did it make?

Timothy's muscles were cramped from sitting all day, and in hindsight, he should have gotten up and taken a little walk, but who had time for a walk with the deadline bearing down on them like a runaway train? He also should have remembered that he was prone to muscle spasms and had to be careful how he moved after being stationary for so long in one place. But he didn't.

Instead he reached over, grabbed the back of Ben's chair, and slid into the seat. It was a big mistake.

The muscle along his shoulder blades tightened like a vise as a pain like a hot poker shot up along his arm. Its intensity launched him out of his chair like a rocket. He shot straight up, hitting his knee on the console with enough force to send the sequentially stacked videocassettes flying in a dozen different directions. He tried to grab them as they flew past, but the movement only worsened the spasm.

"Ouch!"

He straightened up. The pain nailed him again, causing him to lose his balance. He stepped back to try and steady himself. That's when he heard the sickening crunch of plastic underfoot.

At that moment, the control booth door swung open and Ben came marching in. "All right, I talked to Matthew and he says it's not as bad as we thought. What the—" Ben surveyed the carnage. "Second thought, maybe it's worse."

It was five o'clock and the restaurant was packed with customers, most of whom were feasting on one of Harry's two dinner specials, Yankee pot roast or meat loaf. Dozens of separate conversations had turned into one deafening roar, which most of the Saint Cecilia's crowd, seated around their favorite round table, were blissfully unaware of, having turned down their hearing aids. The rest of the room resorted to hand signals.

Wendy noticed the hand motion for "check" by table two. Sheriff Bromley and his wife, Barbara, were Thursday night regulars. The sheriff liked to settle his tab before the show began.

Wendy nodded in their general direction. The couple always ordered the pot roast, so there was nothing to tally. Harry's specials came with everything . . . choice of soup or salad, soft drink, bread, main course, slice of Haddam Hall gingerbread or pie, and coffee, $7.50. She stuffed the bill in her apron pocket and grabbed both coffeepots en route, regular and decaf. A good waitress never wasted any motion; only tonight it was difficult maintaining that sense of professionalism.

Besides her concerns for her niece, she was wondering about her husband's whereabouts. He was supposed to be working overtime at the plant, but when she called to ask him to stop over at Kmart on the way home and pick up some pantyhose, his foreman said he never worked on Thursday nights. Then where had he spent these past few weeks while she was at work?

Folks raised their cups for refills as she threaded through the cluster of wooden tables, coffeepots in hand. Twice she poured regular when asked for decaf. Where was her mind at?

On Harold, that's where, she thought.

"May I have another cup of tea?" Beth Hamilton asked, wearing a sweet smile and Ethel Johnson's recycled sweater. She had pulled it out of this week's sale bin.

Wendy filled her cup with regular coffee.

If Harold was having another affair, there would be no reconciliation this time.

It was five-thirty. They had fifteen minutes left to order before Harry closed the grill.

"May we have a menu?" Sam Rosenberg asked as Wendy flew by with an armful of dirty dishes.

"Us too," Timothy said, including Ben, although both were too keyed up to eat. They hadn't had time to review the finished tape before handing it in. They could only hope for the best, like a power outage.

"The menu hasn't changed since the last time you were here," she told the three men, more brisk than usual. "Harriet, you having the meat loaf?" Harriet always ordered meat loaf.

"That would be lovely, dear," Harriet said, working a stray hair back into her bun. "Oh, and may I have a cup of hot tea?"

"One hot tea and one meat loaf," Wendy repeated, not bothering to write it down. "And you gents? The usual?"

All three nodded in unison.

"Three pot roasts, coming right up."

The bell above the front door rang. George Benson, smelling like an oil drum, sauntered in. Ted tagged behind. Bob Peterson and his daughter Sarah followed closely on their tails.

Lori Peterson stayed late on Thursdays. It was her way of

getting a jump start on the weekend baking. Besides her normal output of pies and cakes, she also supplied the Old Mills Hotel and Conference Center with a weekend assortment of pastries. Guests couldn't seem to get enough of Lori's soft-as-air cinnamon rolls and sticky buns. Barry Hornibrook, owner of the hotel, said her baked goods were the reason he was booked solid most weekends.

The aroma of freshly grated cinnamon wafted through the portal that connected the bakery to the restaurant. Not many folks would leave this evening without placing an order for one of Lori's famous Haddam Hall gingerbread cakes or a maple-syrup-laced apple pie.

"You'd better hurry up," Wendy warned the newcomers. "Grill's closing down in a few minutes."

"Why is everybody always in a rush lately?" George complained, taking a table underneath a side window and throwing his coat and mittens on a nearby chair. "I'll have the meat loaf," George shouted, loud enough to shake the windowpanes.

Chester Platt pulled out a chair. "Did you hear the latest news?"

"What news?"

"Frank Hill just put in an application to join the fire department. He wants to drive the rig."

"Oh geezzzz."

"Who wants a coffee refill? Hold up their cup," Wendy said. "Show starts in ten minutes."

Harry walked out of the kitchen, carrying the TV, the signal that the show was about to begin. Conversation waned as people began scraping chairs along the wooden floor, jockeying for the best view.

"Father James? Would you grab that extension cord and loop it over here?" Harry asked.

Father James was about as coordinated as a new puppy. The continued lack of sleep was really taking its toll. He slid off the stool and tried not to electrocute himself as he slid the brown cord along the wall outlet. Finally, it slipped into place.

"That should do it," he told Harry.

"Thanks, Father."

Fortunately, Father Bob over in Woodbury had offered to take his calls tonight. Maybe without the worry of being disturbed, he might finally be able to fall asleep. In fact, the sensible thing to do would have been to skip Harry's Thursday night fete and go directly to bed. But he was as addicted to Harry's meat loaf as he was to his coffee, and once again had let his stomach dictate his actions. No wonder his forty-inch waistbands were growing too tight.

"Come join us," Harriet called, pulling out a chair.

"Don't mind if I do," he said, gathering his mug of decaf coffee (an indication of how badly he was suffering from insomnia) and heading toward the large round center table. Ben and Timothy made room for him to settle in.

Sam looked him over and frowned. "You look tired. You getting enough sleep?"

As the credits began to roll, *Around the Town*'s theme song filled the restaurant, and conversations quickly died down. The mayor's segment headed up this week's program.

"Several constituents have called to complain about the conditions along Main Street, especially the large pothole in front of Kelly's Bar . . ."

"I heard you nearly lost a muffler when you hit it," postman Charlie Littman shouted across to Bob Peterson.

"Muffler and an exhaust system," Bob corrected.

"I believe it's time to put some of those hard-earned tax dollars to good use and begin repaving."

"Hear, hear!" Harry cheered, placing an arm around the back of his wife Nellie's chair.

"Now as you know, the original road was once set in brick, which is much too expensive to duplicate. Instead, we've decided to resurface the road with asphalt as part of our cost-saving program."

"He can't just blacktop over that lovely brick," said Nigel Hayes, president of the Historical Society. "It's part of historical downtown."

That was the first Father James had heard about a historical designation, but then, he had been in something of a fog lately. And what was considered "downtown"? There was only a quarter of a mile of roadway that ran through the few shops along Main Street.

"What does he mean, 'cost-saving'?" Barry Hornibrook asked the room at large. "How much does it cost to replace a few dozen bricks versus paving an entire strip of road?"

"Certainly a lot less than paving it," George interjected. "Leave it to town officials to find a way to waste our good tax money, which is why you should vote for me next fall."

The room exploded in controversy. Soon everyone was shouting his or her opinion as a heated discussion ensued, drowning out the rest of the mayor's message.

"So far, so good," Timothy said hopefully. Maybe their editing skills weren't all that bad.

"Quiet!" Charlie called out. "The next part is starting."

Timothy's prerecorded voice announced this week's question to the man on the street.

"*What do you do for entertainment during a winter storm?*"

The camera zoomed in on a Hereford grazing in a field as Charlie Littman responded.

"*Mostly, I just like to stay at home. I get enough of the outdoors just walking my route. But my wife here likes to wander along the countryside, regardless of the weather, don't you, dear?*"

Ben's mouth fell open.

The whole room heard Charlie's wife, Norma, suck in her breath. "Did you just call me a cow?"

"No . . . I never said that. Well, I said that but it wasn't . . ."

Norma pushed back her chair, gave him a look that could freeze hell, and stormed out of the restaurant; Charlie quickly followed on her heels.

"Norma . . . I'm telling you it wasn't like that." Charlie paused briefly to glare at Timothy and Ben.

The two men dropped their heads into their hands and moaned.

The camera now panned Mildred Dunlop's place and came to rest on her two dogs, who were madly chasing a rooster and several hens around the backyard, nipping at their feet and barking up a storm. Beth Hamilton, from Secondhand Rose, was saying, "*That last winter storm was so cruel that Bobbie and I closed up shop and spent the day planning our marketing strategy for our big spring sales event. I think we've come up with a unique way to get customers into the store.*"

The dogs were now chasing the rooster into the chicken shed.

There was a slight pause before the room exploded in laughter.

"That's the funniest thing," Harriet told the men, laughing out loud.

The camera shifted onto a pigsty at the back of Platt's farm. Miss Charger, a five-hundred-pound swine who'd won first place in the county fair four years in a row, was wallowing in the mud, rolling back and forth until the thin strip of white that circled round her chest like the icing in an Oreo cookie disappeared. Margaret Norris's voice intoned, *"I started a simple aerobics program. Nothing too strenuous. Isn't it amazing how much weight we girls can put on over the winter?"*

Laughter swelled like a giant wave. Folks clutched their stomachs. George fell out of his chair and crashed to the floor. Even Father James was slowly waking up from his funk and laughing along with everyone else.

"Which one of you thought this thing up?" Harry asked, wiping away the tears of laughter.

"This is a real hoot!" someone shouted.

Ben and Timothy looked around in stunned silence.

"How do I get a copy?" Barry shouted across the restaurant. "I want to send a copy to my cousin Elmer."

Folks were laughing so hard that many didn't hear the fire siren when it began to wail.

George was the town's fire marshal, and his walkie-talkie was directly linked to dispatch. He placed it close to his ear and heard the address. His face turned grim.

He rushed over to Father James. "You'd better come with me. It's the Campbells' place."

Chapter Twelve

𝕮𝕲❦

*A*rlene had been dreaming about a new quilt pattern when the faint strains of Beth Hamilton's voice filtered into her living room. She opened her eyes. A dog was chasing a bunch of chickens on the television.

"Bobbie and I closed up shop and spent the day planning our marketing strategy for our big spring sales event. I think we've come up with a unique way to get customers into the store."

Arlene stared at the TV. She couldn't quite make it all out. What did chickens have to do with a clothing store?

The log cabin quilt she had been working on was still on her lap. She must have dozed off while working on it. She studied the rectangular strips arranged in portions of half light and half dark tones that represented the logs of a cabin. The red square in the center signified the hearth of the home. It was meant for a birthday gift for Sam Rosenberg. He was such a good friend and so generous. His seventy-second birthday was coming up in a couple of months, but at this rate he'd be lucky to receive it when he turned eighty. She still had a long way to go.

The room had grown dark. She reached over and flicked on a light. The lamp's soft glow filled the room with a warm, homey feeling. How long had she been asleep? It must be after dinnertime. It was a wonder that Fred hadn't wakened her. He liked to eat early.

She stretched. How good it had felt to get a little nap. Maybe she'd make Fred his favorite buttermilk biscuits. She went to gather up the quilt when she paused. What was that she smelled? Something burning. Oh, no . . . She tossed the quilt aside and scrambled out of the chair. What if Fred had gone into the kitchen to make himself something to eat? She had repeatedly told him not to use the stove.

"Fred?"

She hurried toward the kitchen door. Smoke was curling up from the floor.

"Fred!"

She threw open the door and was pushed back by a thick wall of black smoke. For one terrifying moment, she couldn't breathe. She fell back into the living room, staring at the kitchen door, uncertain what she should do. What if Fred was trapped inside! She needed help and fast.

There were two phones in the house—a kitchen wall phone and the one by her bedside table. Fighting against a rising sense of panic, she raced into the hallway and stopped. The front door was open. She was certain it had been locked.

"Fred?" She stepped out onto the front porch.

Her breath caught. Her eyes filled with tears of relief.

Fred was seated on a porch rocker, gently rocking back and forth as though he hadn't a care in the world.

George and fire chief Bill Halstead had raced ahead as soon as the alarm had sounded. Father James caught a ride with Chester, who had hoisted him up into the tall rig like a sack of potatoes.

"Hold on, Father," Chester yelled as they flew out of the bay with sirens blaring.

Father James felt as though he were seated on top of the world and had a bird's-eye view as traffic parted in their wake like the Red Sea.

As they went rocketing down country lanes, Father James clung to the dashboard for dear life, marveling once again at the way a priest's day could change on a dime. One minute he had been enjoying a lovely evening at his favorite restaurant and the next he was being hurled through space like a missile.

"Isn't that truck going a little fast?" he asked. The tanker was taking the curves like a racing driver gone mad.

"If he doesn't slow down, he's never going to make the next turn," Chester said, easing his own rig around the same bend at a reasonable rate of speed.

The words proved prophetic. The men watched in open-mouthed horror as the fire engine took out an electric pole, plunging a large portion of Dorsetville into total darkness.

By the time they arrived at the Campbells', the runaway rig was parked in the driveway, a row of privet hedge lay flattened underneath, and there was no evidence of the driver.

"You going to be all right on your own?" Chester asked Father James, flinging open the door.

"Sure, I'll be fine," he said confidently, then stepped out into thin air. Nancy Hawkins caught him on the way down.

"You all right?" she asked.

"Long way off the ground, isn't it?"

"You get used to it," she said, hurrying on with a heavy length of rope slung over her shoulders.

Father James searched the melee for sight of the Campbells, and sighed with relief when he spied them huddled together by a back shed.

"Are you two all right?" he asked, rushing over.

"Yes. We're both fine," Arlene assured him, although by the tense expression on her face, Father James knew that was only partly true.

"I want to go back inside," Fred said, growing increasingly agitated. "I don't like all these people in my yard. Tell them to go away."

"We can't go back until the chief says that it's safe," she told him, patting his arm.

"What happened?" Father James asked.

"I fell asleep watching TV and didn't hear Fred get up from his nap. He must have gone into the kitchen and left a burner on underneath a pan."

"You forgot my dinner. I was making a grilled cheese sandwich," Fred said like a petulant child.

"I'm just thankful that the house didn't burn down around our ears."

Fire chief Billy Halstead walked over. "How are you holding up, Arlene?" he asked, placing a hand on her shoulder.

"We're okay," she said bravely.

"How you doing, Fred?"

"Tell him to go away," he told Arlene.

"Now, Fred, he's come here to help."

"How bad is it?" Father James asked. The couple's home was surrounded by men with long lengths of hose.

"They were lucky. The fire started on the stove, but burnt itself out. There's a lot of smoke damage. Most of it concentrated in the kitchen area. Some in the dining room, but not too bad. The rest of the house is probably going to need a good cleaning as well. I think it wise if Arlene and Fred find another place to stay for a while."

"They can stay with me at the rectory," Father James offered. "Father Dennis is away. There's plenty of room."

"Thank you, Father," Arlene said, nearly collapsing with relief. "I haven't the energy to go looking for a hotel room."

"You're not staying in any hotel," he told her forcefully. "You're staying with me as long as you need."

She smiled gratefully, a single tear sliding gently down her cheek. "I just need to pack a few things."

"It's still not safe to go inside," the chief said. "Tell me what you need, and I'll have Nancy run in and get it."

Chief Halstead's portable radio emitted some unintelligible words that only he seemed able to decipher. "Excuse me." He moved a few paces away.

"Yeah? Okay, send the tanker back to the base. Oh, and make sure the idiot who drove it over here doesn't get back behind the wheel. It was who? Who gave Hill permission to drive a rig?"

By the time his houseguests were settled in, it was after midnight, and Father James was nearly comatose. He feared that if he didn't get at least a few hours' sleep, there would be some serious consequences.

Yesterday he had completely lost his train of thought during the homily. If it hadn't been for Harriet leaning over the front pew and whispering where he had left off, he might still be circling round the subject, unable to find a perch. That incident had happened on four hours' sleep. The good Lord only knew what would happen on none.

Outside, a sharp wind lashed at the corner of the upstairs dormer and cut across the edge of the house, whistling a melancholy tune. In concert, a shutter began to bang out a steady rhythm, like a kettledrum in a macabre symphony. Strange and eerie, yet a fitting melody that seemed to score the storms that had lashed out at his flock of parishioners.

Dexter still lay in a coma. The week Dr. Noiyst had negotiated with the neurologist was nearly over. Father James feared that there would be no recourse left to the family if the hospital sought that court order.

And now the Campbells.

The illuminated dial of his Westclox, a relic from his college days, showed the minutes ticking away. He turned on his side so he couldn't see the face of the clock—which only caused him anxiety—and began to count backward.

One hundred . . . 99 . . . 98 . . . 97 . . . 96 . . .

A tree limb lashed against the side of the house; there was a loud *snap* and then a *thud*. The maple tree must have lost another limb. He should have had the tree removed before the winter months set in. One of the church old-timers called it a "widow maker," and parishioners, he noticed, gave it a wide berth. It was probably also the reason no one mowed beneath it last summer. But cutting down a tree always saddened him. It felt akin to putting down a beloved pet.

Thankfully, things quieted down outside. He resumed his counting.

Ninety-five . . . 94 . . . 93 . . . 92 . . .

What was Arlene to do? After tonight's incident, it was clear that she could not handle Fred alone. He could have easily burned down the house with her in it.

Then his thoughts slid over to Rodney, and then on to the Lenten season, which he hadn't begun to prepare for, and then to Doc Hammon. On and on his thoughts circled like a whirlwind.

By 3 A.M., he gave up all hope of getting any sleep and grabbed his worn copy of *Stillmeadow Farm*, fluffed up a pillow, and began to read.

Gladys Taber's writing always evoked memories of his childhood in a small New England farming community. But tonight her gentle prose and hilarious word pictures couldn't hold his attention. His thoughts kept sliding off the page. Finally he put it down.

What was going on? He had never had trouble sleeping before. In fact, just the opposite was true. He had once fallen asleep during a Steve Martin movie that normally made him laugh until he cried. So why was he having trouble now?

A saying his grandfather often quoted came to mind. "A soul at peace with God knows no unrest." Was that it? Had he lost his peace?

Peace. He hadn't had much of that lately, that was for sure. It seemed as though troubles circled around his flock like a hawk its prey. Their problems were never far from his thoughts. What could he do to help lighten their load? Had he prayed hard enough? Was there something he had left undone? Why wasn't God responding to his requests for intervention?

As the predawn light softly illuminated his room, light was shed on his dilemma as well. God had been taking care of man and his problems for millennia. He was a pro at leading folks through the valleys. And even if it seemed a circuitous route at times, we shouldn't worry. God knew the way.

In the end, the answer was simple, as it always was. Father James had forgotten to *rest* in the Lord.

Hill's spirits soared like a helium balloon on a clear day as he stepped out from the Country Kettle's front door with a cup of steaming hot chocolate and a smile as big as the state of Texas stretched across his face. He was now a full-fledged volunteer fireman!

"Hello, Judge Peale," he said, passing him on the street. "Sure is a great day!"

"Nice hat, Miss Hamilton," he said, saluting Beth as he strolled past Secondhand Rose.

Ahhhhh . . . life was good and getting better every day, and he owed it all to Tapping the Power Within.

This past segment had been especially powerful.

"You must tithe your time as well as your wealth, and when you do, the universe pays back tenfold."

It had taken him a while to figure out how he was supposed to go about tithing his time. Not that he had a lot of it. He was still working hard on his detective skills. If they had been better honed, he might have found Rodney Gallagher right off. But at least the boy had been found. Next time, however, Hill would be ready.

Then he happened to pass the fire station and saw a sign that Chester Platt had just posted outside: *Come Join Our Team as a Volunteer Fireman.* He walked right in and got an application, and now he was a full-fledged member, with the proviso that he not drive any more rigs.

Yep, life was good. He had taken control of his mind, and

as Rich Malone had said, *"The physical world is only a reflection of our inner spiritual state."* Well, he must be in pretty good shape because things were starting to look awfully good.

He punched the Play button on the portable cassette player as he sallied forth along Main Street, waving and smiling at everyone he met.

"Tape eight . . . The Power of Positive Speech . . . Making the things we require materialize through statements of purpose . . ."

As Hill turned right onto Linden Street, he wondered how long it might take him to make sergeant, now that he knew how to *tap the power within.* After all, sergeant was only one step removed from a full-fledged detective.

Chapter Thirteen

*F*ather James had been putting on his socks when Mrs. Norris summoned him from the bottom of the back staircase.

"Pick up the phone, Father James. Doc Hammon's on the line. He can't talk long, so he says to hurry."

He dove for the phone. "Hello, old friend," he sang. "You're the last voice I expected to hear this morning. I thought Joan had your phone disconnected."

"She did. I borrowed a cell phone from the guy across the hall. He was just wheeled down to surgery. He won't miss it. Now quick, before one of those pesky nurses trots in, bring me up to speed about the Campbells' house fire."

Father James feigned ignorance. "Fire?"

"Good try, Jim, but it's not going to work. Tom Chute mentioned it this morning on his radio program."

"Oh, that fire? It really wasn't a fire. Just some smoke damage."

"How did it start?"

"Someone left a pan on the stove."

"And let me guess. Fred was the someone?"

"Well, er . . ."

"I warned Arlene that things were only going to get worse. For her own safely, she has to put Fred in a nursing home. You've got to talk to her, Jim. I know she has her mind set against it, but she can't keep sticking her head in the sand. Besides, she has high blood pressure. A few more scares like this and she's likely to have a stroke. Then who would take care of Fred? Where are they now?"

"Staying with me."

"That's good. With Mrs. Norris there, it will give her a needed rest. Of course, it won't do much for your insomnia. By the way, how is that doing?"

"About the same—but back to the Campbells. I'll see what I can do to convince Arlene to start looking for a nursing home, and I'll give Dr. Noiyst a call. She seems to trust him. Maybe he can convince her."

"Darn sticky time to be laid up in bed," Doc swore. "So, how's he doing?"

"Who? Oh, your replacement? Fine. Everyone seems to like him immensely. I know that he's been a great comfort to the Gallaghers."

"Any change in Dexter's condition? Joan won't tell me a thing, and she's got all the staff here just as tight-lipped. They won't even let me read the newspaper. I only heard Tom Chute's radio broadcast this morning because I happened to be passing the nurses' lounge en route to the showers. It's a darn conspiracy, that's what it is."

"I'm afraid his condition remains unchanged."

"Darn shame. It makes me sick just thinking about it. How's Rodney taking it?"

"Not good. He ran away from school the first day back."

"That doesn't surprise me. Dexter was the leader of the pack. He must be lost without him."

"Sam Rosenberg has taken him under his wing, trying to keep him busy until the worst of this is over. Rodney goes along with him on meal runs. Sam's become sort of a surrogate grandfather."

"Good old Sam. I don't know what Dorsetville would do without him."

"Or you," Father James added. He missed this dear old friend. "Now hang up and get back into bed before Joan fingers me as a snitch."

As soon as the breakfast dishes had been set to dry in the draining board, Mrs. Norris handed Arlene her coat and purse and told her to take a few hours off.

"I can handle Fred," she said as Arlene started to protest. "Don't forget, I took care of Father Keene for years, and let me tell you, if I can watch over a man who talked to angels as though they were right there in the room, I can take care of your Fred. So go. Take a walk," she insisted, helping Arlene on with her coat. "Stop off at the Country Kettle for a cup of tea. Talk to some friends. Folks around town haven't seen you in ages."

Before Arlene knew it, she had been shooed out the front door with instructions not to return for several hours.

She was about to walk right back inside and flatly state that she could not burden Mrs. Norris with Fred's care when she had second thoughts. When was the last time she had seen Margaret Norris unable to cope? With anything? And Fred did still remember her. That was a plus. She could use a few hours for herself, and Margaret had offered.

With a strange mixture of misgiving and elation, she started down the flagstone path, feeling like a mother whose last child had just started school. When was the last time she had experienced such freedom? Margaret might not know this, but she had given her the most precious gift imaginable. Time alone, unencumbered.

Slowly, the remnants of the woman who had once been so carefree and insuppressibly cheerful began to surface. Even though the skies were tinted gray and the wind carried a slight chill, she felt as gay as spring. A new lightness filled her step; joy bubbled up in her soul as the heavy burdens she had borne these past few months began to lift.

Margaret had been right. A few hours alone without the constant strain of Fred's care was the panacea her soul had craved. And even though she must eventually go back to resume the increasingly complex role of caretaker, she was determined to enjoy the simple pleasure of being free for these short, glorious hours.

She found herself humming as she headed down the steep hill that ran parallel to the town green and past the Congregational church. A light was on in the kitchen of the white clapboard Victorian rectory, and the smell of cinnamon was in the air.

What delicacies was Emily Curtis cooking up for her television show? Arlene wondered. She watched it faithfully every week and collected all of Emily's delicious recipes. Maybe someday when she wasn't so tired, she might try a few.

She paused to admire the new white picket fence that now encased Valerie Kilbourne's front yard. When had that gone up? Sadly, she realized that she had missed a lot of things these last few months, like solitary walks, or cups of tea and hot buttered scones shared with a neighbor or friend. In deference to Fred's condition, people tended to stay away now, unless invited. She had always enjoyed that unexpected knock on the kitchen door and the surprise of opening it, like a gift at Christmas, to find a dear friend wanting to share a newly arrived letter or a quilt project.

She recalled daily mass followed by coffee at the Country Kettle, bingo on Tuesday nights, and quilting groups and fall and spring festivals, and church suppers. And at all of those events, Fred was with her, holding her hand, sharing the simple pleasures that make country living so special.

She missed the man she had married over forty years ago. They had grown so close over the years that at times it was hard to separate one from the other. The same things made them laugh. They enjoyed the same books and movies. And as the years had gathered like moss, they shared a rich cache of memories.

That was the hardest thing to lose. The Alzheimer's had eaten away at Fred's mind, reducing a journal of shared moments into a single line on a blank page. Sadly, she could no longer turn to him and say, "Remember when . . . ?"

She felt a catch in her throat and hot tears sprang to her eyes. She missed her Fred dearly. It pained her to look into his eyes and see only a vacant stare, all sparks of recognition fading like embers. How long, she wondered, before she, too, was lost in that black abyss?

She had mentioned this to Dr. Noiyst. She had been so concerned over that first appointment, but discovered she hadn't needed to worry. He had proved to be a gentle and compassionate man who treated her husband as tenderly as one would a child. Fred had taken to him right away.

Later, as Shirley watched over Fred, Arlene consulted with Dr. Noiyst. He apprised her of the advancement of the disease, and they discussed various medications to help Fred sleep and reduce his periods of anxiety.

Then he slid forward in his chair and asked her gently, "How are you doing under all of this?"

She tried to speak and found she couldn't find her voice, then dissolved in a river of tears.

He slid over a box of Kleenex.

"My Fred was always such a smart man. He was very clever with his hands, especially about mechanical things. He could fix anything. He just seemed to know how things worked." Meeting Dr. Noiyst's eyes, she added, "But now he's like a child."

"Do you believe in God, Mrs. Campbell?"

She nodded.

"Then you know that our loving Father would not abandon your husband. In fact, he is using this disease to prepare him for the next step."

"Next step?"

"Jesus said that in order for us to enter the kingdom of God, we must become as little children," he said softly. "In some respects, certain illnesses, such as Alzheimer's, ready the patient for life's final journey."

She recalled that conversation often. It gave her great comfort. Now, instead of viewing Alzheimer's as the Black Reaper, thrashing away at Fred's mind, she saw the gentle hand of God, helping Fred to rediscover the simplicity of childhood in preparation for his final, heaven-bound journey. It still didn't take away the pain of watching her husband's mind slowly fade, but it did give her something to cling to during the difficult days, which lately were rapidly increasing.

She reached Main Street. Now which way should she go? Up the hill toward Town Hall? She could drop in and see Betty. Or head down the hill past Secondhand Rose and have a little something to eat at the Country Kettle?

Filled with sudden indecision, she stood, looking from side to side.

"Hello, Mrs. Campbell," Deputy Hill called from across the street as he placed a parking ticket on the windshield of a 1997 Corolla. It was his third violation this week. He lived for these moments.

"How is your husband?"

"He's fine," she called back. "Thank you for your help the other night."

"Just doing what we firemen are trained to do," he said, before resuming his patrol.

Funny, she hadn't known that Deputy Hill was a volunteer fireman. That just went to prove how distant she had become from the everyday goings-on around town.

How thankful she had been for the fire department's quick response. And she owed the Lord a thank-you, too. If she hadn't awakened when she did, the house could have gone up in smoke, and she and Fred along with it. It was another strong indication that she was ill-equipped to provide him with the supervision his condition warranted. As much as she might protest, it seemed that a nursing home was the only answer— but how could she go back on her word?

Father James had challenged her on this account this morning. He had taken her into his study before breakfast and offered to make an appointment for her to visit Glen Oaks.

"I'll go with you and we'll see what it's like. Maybe if you

met the staff and toured the facilities, you might not be so opposed to the idea," he said encouragingly.

"It has nothing to do with facilities. It has to do with a
promise. I gave my solemn oath."

"Perhaps doing what is best for Fred is a stronger indication
of your love than honoring a promise that could never have
foreseen the future," he said, softly.

He was right, of course. Not that the thought helped to as-
suage her guilty conscience. After all, a promise was a promise.

The elation she had felt just moments ago began to dissi-
pate. The full weight of Fred's illness returned. What was she
to do?

Deep in thought, she headed down the hill with no destina-
tion in mind. Judge Peale slowed his Cadillac DeVille and
rolled down the window. "Good to see you out and about, Arlene. The missus and I are praying for you and Fred."

She smiled and waved. "Thank you," she called, then resumed her walk.

Clearly something had to be done about Fred. She couldn't
go on caring for him alone, and there was only so much help
one could accept from friends. Why had God allowed this to
happen? she wondered. And where was he in the midst of this
burdensome trial? She had prayed fervently for months for his
intervention, yet none came. Why had he turned a deaf ear to
her pleas?

Slowly, drifting down through the years like a long-forgotten
melody, she heard the soft refrains of a conversation she had
once shared with her grandmother Hattie.

It had been a somber winter day. The sky was filled with
wisps of low-flying clouds, the landscape stark and barren.

"I wish winter would leave and never come back again," she

had told Hattie, perched on a window seat, her nose pressed up against the cold pane of glass.

As a child, Arlene found winter days monotonous. She longed for an end to the lingering dark nights, for rays of the pale pink light of spring, the freedom of running barefoot again. She missed the sound of the geese that swam in the pond behind the barn; the soft smell of violets that grew along the stone wall; and the peepers' song that lulled her to sleep at night.

Her grandmother came and settled beside her.

"Without winter, we would miss discovering the secret things," Hattie whispered in her ear.

"Secret things?" she had asked eagerly. "Secret" spoke of mystery and treasures. She was instantly intrigued.

Hattie scooped her up into her arms and pointed through the thick pane of glass.

"Do you see the pathway that winds around the back of the mountain?"

"Yes, Grandma. I can see it."

"Well, in the summer, it's completely covered over with brush. I bet you didn't even know it was there, did you?"

She shook her head, no.

"But when winter comes and the leaves die off, it's much easier to spot. Later, we'll put on your thick woolen hat and mittens and take a walk."

"Where does the path lead, Grandmother?"

"To the top of a high ridge, and that overlooks the entire town. I wager that it's the most beautiful view in the entire country, and one that we would never have discovered with the thick cover of leaves."

Arlene tried to imagine standing high above the town and watching the village below. Cars making their way along Main

Street, avoiding the Marcus Dairy cart; Mr. Platt pulling up his wagon to the back door of Stone's and loading bags of oats and grain for his horse and cows. It was called Stone's Feed Store back then.

Hattie drew her close and explained. "It's like our journey of faith. When life strips us bare of all our resources, when our world turns dark and gray, it allows us to see God's hidden treasures that were there all along."

Arlene paused briefly outside Secondhand Rose to revisit that long-forgotten lesson. But what treasures could possibly be unearthed now in the barren landscapes of her world? she wondered.

Dear Grandmother, she silently prayed, *when you prayed with me as a child, I always felt there was hope. Your trust in God's faithfulness could help lift me above any of life's storms. If only I knew that your prayers were joined with mine now, I know that I could get through this.*

"Yoo-hoo, Arlene." Beth Hamilton waved from the front doorway of her shop. "Come inside and join Bobbie and me for a cup of tea. We were just about to put the kettle on."

The shop had always been her favorite place to browse, and the Hamilton sisters were a great source for town gossip. How many happy hours had she frittered away in their store?

"I'd love to," Arlene said, following her inside. This was just the kind of diversion she needed to get her thoughts back on track and out of the dumps.

"Let me take your coat," Beth said, running her hand along a sleeve. "Is this mohair? Well, you know where to bring it when you're tired of wearing it."

Folks often said that the Hamilton sisters would take the coat right off your back if they thought it would sell. Arlene laughed out loud, feeling her troubles momentarily drop away like autumn leaves in the wind.

"Bobbie and I heard about the fire. It must have been horrible."

"It could have been worse," Arlene replied, watching Beth make room for her coat on the reduced sales rack. She hoped someone didn't mistake it for a sales item.

"How bad was it?"

"Just a lot of smoke damage. The kitchen got the worst of it. The stove will have to be replaced, as well as the linoleum. But everything else just needs a good cleaning. Chester Platt was able to find a company that specializes in this sort of thing. They should be finished by tomorrow. The painters are scheduled to begin the next day. So, with any amount of luck, Fred and I should be back in our home by the end of next week."

Arlene spied a lovely floral sweater and couldn't resist the urge to walk over and examine it up close.

"Angels must have been watching over both of you. I shudder to think what could have happened if you hadn't caught it when you did," Beth said, redirecting her attention onto the sweater. "Try it on. That soft pink goes beautifully with your complexion. Gracie Abbott dropped it off yesterday. You know, she told me it has been three years since she started working at the cable station. Where does the time go? Now turn around and let me have a look. Perfect."

Arlene viewed herself in the full-length mirror. She thought so too.

"I'll take it."

"Is that our dear friend Arlene Campbell?" Bobbie said, rushing from the back room with open arms. "How are you, my dear? We've been worried sick since we heard about the fire. Thank God you're both all right. Now tell me, how is our Fred?" Bobbie always referred to folks as "our."

"He's as good as can be expected. Margaret is watching him. I'm blessed to have so many wonderful friends."

"And those friends are praying up a storm for you," Bobbie said, squeezing her hand. "Our Reverend Curtis always says that intercessory prayers are the wings beneath our trials. Isn't that the cutest saying?"

"I've invited Arlene to tea," Beth said, placing the *We're in the Back* sign next to the register.

"Wonderful!" Bobbie said, linking her arm through Arlene's and leading her toward the back room. "I can't wait to catch you up on all the gossip. There's so much going on in Dorsetville these days that I don't know where to begin."

"You mean there's more news other than the Gallagher twins?"

"Isn't that a God-awful shame?" Bobbie said sadly, shaking her head. "Harriet was in the other day dropping off a box of sweaters her granddaughter sent along from New York."

"They're from Bloomingdale's," Beth added almost reverently. Ladies in town shopped at Kmart and Sears.

"Harriet had just gotten back from the hospital," Bobbie continued.

"The church ladies in town work it so someone's always with Lorraine in case she needs a break," Beth picked up.

"Anyway," Bobbie went on, "Lorraine told her that the doctors were only giving Dexter another week and if he didn't improve, they will be forced to take him off the respirator. Doesn't that make you just want to cry? So we called our Reverend Curtis right away and told him to have everyone step up their prayers.

"Now you sit down here," she said, removing a box of winter mittens and scarves from the small wooden table that had a charming view of the river.

Arlene chose the chair nearest the window and asked, "What else is new?"

"Well, for starters," Beth began, taking down a china cup from the shelf above the hot plate.

"Wendy's niece, Harvest, has moved to town. She's staying with Wendy and Harold," Bobbie explained. "She's in her early twenties and has long blond hair and the cutest button nose."

"She's just started working at Tri Town, and from what I hear, she's very good." Beth held up two tea bags. "Regular or decaf?"

"Decaf," Arlene told her.

The sisters chattered on, interrupting each other to add details. Arlene settled back and let their voices wash over her, enjoying the simple pleasure of their company. They went on to relay that Mildred Dunlop had bought a new car; Barry Hornibrook was thinking about holding summer concerts by the river near his hotel; the mayor needed a root canal; and Mary Pritchett had just received a letter from her sister, the missionary in Honduras, saying that she was engaged to marry one of the locals.

Arlene felt her spirits renew. She hadn't realized how starved she had been for conversation.

"Can I do anything?" she asked, watching Beth take out creamers and fill the sugar bowl.

"Not a thing. Just sit there and relax," Beth insisted. She held a tea cup up to the light and examined the chip on the handle. "I wish we had had time to unpack the tea service that just arrived."

"Tea set?" Arlene asked.

"It's the most beautiful service we've ever received," Beth exclaimed. "I'm going to hate to see it go."

"Take a look yourself," Bobbie said, setting out the spoons and forks. "It's in that barrel in the far corner. It belonged to Mrs. Holmes. You know her, don't you? She's the old woman who lives alone in that monstrosity of a white elephant on the north side of town. George says it has twenty-three rooms, and Mrs. Hastings, her housekeeper, swears that it's haunted. Anyway, her chauffeur brought it around yesterday afternoon. Beth and I haven't had a chance to unpack all of it."

The teakettle began to whistle as Arlene cleared away the packing material, feeling like an explorer in search of treasure. She carefully removed layer after layer of straw until the faint outline of a delicately shaped tea spout came into view.

"It can't be," she whispered.

"Can't be what?" Bobbie asked, setting out three cake plates.

"This is my grandmother's missing tea set," she whispered, carefully removing a porcelain teapot.

But how could this be? The sisters rushed over and she pointed out the fleur-de-lis painted on the bottom.

She collapsed into a chair and cried tears of joy.

Decades ago, her grandmother had been made to part with the tea set, something that had been very precious to her; and to a young child, it had appeared that God had been indifferent to her grandmother's request.

But God saw down through the years and knew that someday Arlene would need the comfort, a sign that her grandmother was still interceding on her behalf, and what better way to confirm it than by sending back the tea set that had been so dearly cherished and lost so long ago?

Chapter Fourteen

❦❧

*R*odney *looked like a raft lost at sea,* seated alone in the metal chair outside the Intensive Care Unit. He was bravely trying not to cry in front of Mr. Rosenberg, knowing that in a few minutes the doctors were going to disconnect Dexter from the respirator, and then he would die.

"You can go, now," Rodney told him, keeping his eyes glued on the floor tiles. Mr. Rosenberg had driven him over. "My parents will be out soon."

"You sure? I don't mind staying."

He shook his head. "No, I'll be all right."

"Then I think I'll go downstairs and wait for Father James."

He nodded again, keeping his eyes cast down. He waited until Mr. Rosenberg was safely inside the elevator before offering up another prayer.

Please, God, don't let Dexter die. I promise to be good. No more stink bombs in the girls' bathroom, and I'll never fill the bottle of sacramental wine with water again.

Rodney had been plea-bargaining with God for hours but God was still not responding, and time was running out.

"Your brother's going to be all right," Dr. Noiyst said.

Rodney looked up. Funny, he hadn't seen him coming down the hall.

"I wish there was something I could do," the boy said, fighting back the tears.

"You already have," the physician said gently. "You've been praying."

Rodney folded his arms and grew defensive. "A fat lot of good that does."

"You would be surprised how much power your prayers possess."

Rodney looked at him suspiciously. "Oh yeah?"

Dr. Noiyst knelt down, eye level with the boy. "As soon as you began to pray, heaven's halls filled with the intercessory prayers of saints. Together they will help sustain your brother. There . . . can you hear it?" He turned an ear toward heaven and smiled.

"Good news, Rodney. The saints here on earth have just been summoned to pray. Now things will start to happen," he said with a twinkle in his eyes.

Harriet bent over a row of Martha Washington geraniums. The seeds of just a few weeks ago were now bursting out of their containers. She should have been pleased, but instead she thought about the countless hours it would take to repot them. She'd already been at it for hours and hadn't made a dent.

Ohhhhh . . . her aching back. She straightened up slowly. She was getting too old to run a nursery. It was the heating pad and Ben-Gay tonight. But she did love working in the soil, feeling its rich texture beneath her hands, watching things grow. It must be in her blood.

Her father had started the business right after World War II. She had taken it over when he died, and now she and her granddaughter Allison ran it. She was so proud of Allison, who had turned this humble family business into a highly successful mail-order company. In a way, though, it saddened her. She liked things just as they were, small, intimate. Maybe it was time to retire and let Allison take over, she thought, working the crick out of her back. Weren't these supposed to be her golden years, a time for taking it easy, not increasing her workload?

She removed her gloves, using a forearm to push a strand of gray hair out of her eyes, and decided to call it quits. What she needed was a hot cup of tea and a warm slice of the lemon bread with a crisp sugar shell that she had baked earlier. She might even add a dollop of the cream that had been delivered fresh that morning by Marcus Dairy. Let Doc Hammon continue to harangue her about high cholesterol. Life was too short to forgo all small pleasures.

Thoughts of Doc made her smile. She had spoken with Joan this morning. She complained that her husband was driving the hospital staff crazy.

"Do you know that he managed to get his hands on a cell phone and has been calling all over town checking up on his patients?"

As a matter of fact, she did. He had called her about her thyroid medicine.

Harriet grabbed her old L.L.Bean Adirondack barn coat

and was headed back toward the house when she felt the familiar call to prayer. She grew very still. Who was it that needed intercession?

The answer came quickly and decisively.

Dexter Gallagher.

In fact, it seemed that people all over Dorsetville were receiving the same summons.

Mother Superior had been in the midst of balancing the retirement home's ledgers, a chore that gave her as much pleasure as a root canal, when she felt a strange sense of urgency fall like a shadow over her soul. An image of Dexter Gallagher began to form in her mind.

Wasting no time, she pushed back her chair and headed toward the chapel.

"What is it?" Sister Claire asked as her prioress rushed by.

"Alert the sisters. God has called us to pray for Dexter Gallagher, and apparently it is urgent."

Ethel was cleaning out her refrigerator when God's message came. She paused with a package of frozen chicken breasts in her hand and began to fervently intercede on Dexter's behalf.

Lori Peterson had just put an amaretto sponge cake in one of the large bakery ovens when she felt the Lord tap her on the shoulder. She set the timer and pulled out her rosary.

In the downstairs lobby, near Mercy Hospital's main entrance, Sam sat tucked in the corner, wedged in a blue vinyl chair, watching a steady stream of people flood in and out the revolving doors.

A man carrying a teddy bear and a broad smile headed toward the elevator as a young woman with a tear-stained face rushed over to the information desk. It was like watching the circle of life, he thought. Life and death, joy and sorrow.

Sam's thoughts went back to Rodney. He and the boy had grown close over the last few days, and he knew that the child still blamed himself for Dexter's condition. Mostly he felt guilty for having survived. Sam knew that guilt well.

As a young man came through the hospital door, pushing a child in a wheelchair, Sam offered a silent prayer, asking the spirits of his dead ancestors to pray for the boy and his family; and when the time came, to help Dexter find his way to God's throne. Then he got up to greet Father James, who had just arrived, carrying his black satchel.

Mike sat on the edge of the bed, watching his wife's face racked with pain.

"We love you. We love you," she repeated over and over again to their unresponsive son.

Mike turned away, glancing at the clock. The hospital staff would soon be here to turn off the respirator. Father James had called from downstairs. He was on his way up. The staff was waiting for him to arrive.

Mike ran a hand through his gray-tinted hair and thought how glad he would be when it was over. It was a terrible admission to make, but true. He couldn't go on, watching his son shriveling away, knowing that even if through some miracle he did come out of the coma, he would be nothing more than a vegetable. That's what the doctors said. No, it was better to let him go.

This day seemed endless. It began early this morning when he had slipped over to Linden's Funeral Home. Jason Linden, a fellow Knight of Columbus, had met him at the front door.

They filled out paperwork and Mike signed checks. Then Jason ushered him in the back toward the casket display, where he had picked out a plain white casket with blue satin lining. It had cost $850. Other funeral fees were being paid by Knights.

Then he had gone home to pick out a burial outfit. He had chosen a pair of jeans, a pullover shirt, and Dexter's Red Sox cap. Dexter seldom went anywhere without it. Before closing the door to his room, he grabbed his son's hockey stick. Dexter would have wanted to be buried with it.

They should be coming soon. Mike looked at his watch. Five minutes left. Soon the doctors would turn off the machine and Dexter would take his last breath.

He turned back toward the window, digging deep for whatever was left of his courage. He must be strong for his wife and Rodney. If he could just get through the next few days, the worst would be over, or so he hoped.

Dr. Noiyst walked through the drawn curtains. No words were exchanged. Mike looked up into his face and found a curious sense of peace flood through his troubled soul.

"Why don't you two go outside and comfort Rodney?" Dr. Noiyst finally told them. "I'll stay here with Dexter until Father James arrives. I promise I won't allow anyone to disconnect his respirator while you're gone."

Mike nodded once more, then reached over for his wife and helped her to her feet.

"Hold his hand," she told Dr. Noiyst on the way out. "He likes it when you hold his hand."

Dexter waded into the river, his eyes riveted on the ball field. It was the coolest thing he had ever seen. Players seemed to hover over bases as they waited for the next play, like a helicopter above a landing pad. Rodney was never going to believe this!

Rodney . . .

Thoughts of his brother brought him back to last year's Fourth of July picnic. He and his dad had just won the three-legged race. Rodney was bummed because he had gotten stuck with Father James. Boy, that man needed some serious training. He couldn't run worth a hill of beans.

When no one was watching, they stole large chunks of watermelon and climbed up one of the big maple trees to rain seeds down on unsuspecting folks as they passed by.

"Come on," a boy yelled from across the stream, hands cupped around his mouth. "We need another outfielder."

The river felt cool rushing past his bare feet. He watched the kids gather into teams. Gee, that game sure looked like fun, but something held him back.

What had Jennie said?

Once you cross over, you can't ever go back again.

He didn't mind being here—in fact, it was kind of cool—but without Rodney it was also lonely. As much as he would have liked to stay, he decided he'd come back another time, when Rodney could come along, too. With that thought, he turned and headed back the way he had come.

Nurse Holstein had been sipping a cup of mocha latte, wishing that it had been laced with whiskey. In a few minutes, Dr. Iannini would arrive to turn off the Gallagher boy's respirator. There was nothing harder on the staff than losing a child.

The boy's EEG monitor blipped, and she jumped.

"What the heck?"

She gave the unit a little tap. Another *blip* sounded. Then another. *Blip . . . blip . . . blip . . .*

What was going on? She put down her coffee.

"Julie, watch things here while I check on something," she told her coworker.

She had just bought a new pair of shoes, and their thick rubber soles squeaked as she headed toward the far end of the unit. She expected to find a loose wire or a faulty monitor. But whatever it was, she needed to fix it before the parents returned and thought their son had come to life. That would have been cruel.

With practiced efficiency, she drew the curtain aside and headed straight toward the monitor when she saw the respirator hose draped across the oxygen unit.

"Dear Mother of God."

Someone had already removed the boy's respirator tube, yet the boy was breathing on his own.

By the next day, the whole town was buzzing. Dexter was breathing on his own. It was a miracle. Hopes soared for the boy's recovery as Father James cautioned everyone to step up their prayers and pray *without ceasing* for God to provide a complete recovery. Dexter was still not out of the woods, he warned.

Father James clambered down the back staircase that morning and fairly skipped into the kitchen, as hungry as a lumberjack. God had taken the collective prayers of his people and forged a miracle. He could still see Mike and Lorraine's rapturous look of joy. He wished he had had a camera.

"Good morning, Mrs. Norris, and if you please, I'll have a supersize mug of coffee this morning," he said, pulling out a chair, adding, "high-test." No decaf today. This called for a celebration.

His housekeeper lifted an eyebrow. "You'll regret it when your intestines turn to mush," she said, but grabbed the Pyrex pot without further comment.

Father James was in such high spirits that neither Mrs. Norris's continued mention of his intimate body functions nor George Benson's presence as he crashed through the back door could dampen his mood.

Mrs. Norris, however, was not in a similar state of mind. "Close the door. We're not heating up the whole outside," she wailed at George.

George could have volleyed back with a dozen retorts, but this morning he chose to remain silent. The smell of johnny-cakes and the knowledge that it didn't pay to argue with Mrs. Norris if you hoped for an invite to breakfast kept him quiet.

As though reading his mind, Mrs. Norris told him to take a seat. "And mind your manners. Put a piece of newspaper over that chair cushion. I don't want any oil stains on my clean cushions."

George obeyed, as docile as a child.

"And Father, tuck that napkin up around your chin. It took me half a day to get the last coffee stain out of your white collar."

The men exchanged knowing glances. *Women.* When it was all said and done, they always had the last word, so why argue? Father James offered George the sports section of the morning's paper.

Mrs. Norris placed a heaping plateful of crispy fried corn cakes on the table. The men closed their eyes and inhaled deeply.

"You've outdone yourself again," Father James said. He could already taste them.

Quick as lightning, George speared a stack, reached across the table, and nearly snatched the pitcher of prized syrup right out of Father James's hand, then proceeded to pour half of its contents all over his plate. The priest tried to hide his annoyance. John Walsh had brought that over especially for him. It was the first batch of the season, referred to as "first run." It was skimmed right off the top and was as costly as liquid gold, and George was using it like water!

"You need some of this?" George asked, passing the pitcher.

Father James looked inside. It was more than half gone. Blast that man.

"I hope you don't mind if I eat and run," George said, in between mouthfuls.

Not at all, Father James thought.

"I have an errand to run." He was due in court about his license. This morning he had had to hail a ride over from his place from the Marcus milkman. Being without a license had been rough. "Pass me the cream, will you, Father?"

George paused briefly to shovel sugar into his coffee, eyeing the last three johnnycakes.

"Ted's meeting me here around nine. We'll finish fitting the pipes behind Saint Anthony's niche, and then the mason can come in and seal things up. I'll have to move that bank of candles off to the side. That all right with you?"

Father James had just starting stuffing the last few morsels on his plate into his mouth and couldn't reply. He nodded, yes. He would be darned if he was going to let George get the rest of those cakes. The race was on.

He had just swallowed the last bite when George reached over and snagged every last one of them. The priest looked at him with a dark eye.

"Any more syrup?" George asked Mrs. Norris.

She refilled the pitcher with the last drop of Father James's coveted syrup.

"When will the repairs be done?" Father asked, curtly.

"A couple of days. Maybe less," George said, chewing loudly. "Mrs. Norris, you make the best johnnycakes in the county. Even Mrs. Ebb's, over at the First Baptist Church, can't hold a candle to these."

Mrs. Norris smiled with enormous satisfaction. "There's three left on the stove. Let me get them for you."

"Bye, Aunt Wendy," Harvest called, dashing out the side door.

The screen door banged. Seconds later, the crunch of gravel sounded as her niece backed her car out of the driveway and headed off to work. The house was now silent. Harold had left for work a few hours ago.

Wendy tightened her robe, poured herself a second cup of coffee, and headed out to the sun porch. A strong light from the four large double-pane windows streamed in from the east, heating the terra-cotta tiles and creating a cozy warmth beneath her slippered feet. The space had once been an open porch, fine for entertaining on summer evenings but useless the rest of the year. Two years ago, the couple had hired Chester to turn it into a sunroom. It had been worth every penny. It had since become their favorite spot in the house.

She had filled the space with antique wicker furniture and hordes of large, leafy plants, and a jasmine she'd purchased at Harriet's nursery that filled the room with its luscious scent. She had deliberately left the windows curtainless, preferring an unobstructed view of the hills and forest toward the rear of the property and, in the summer, the flower garden that ringed an outside patio. As far as privacy was concerned, they were unconcerned. Behind them were thousands of acres of conservation land owned by the Holmes Memorial Foundation.

She sipped her coffee as a squirrel scurried up the trunk of the large shaggy bark oak tree that stood next to the flagstone patio. Yesterday she had hung a suet cage on a lower branch. She had purchased it along with a fifty-pound bag of wild-bird seed at Stone's. Mark said the cage was squirrel-proof, but apparently the squirrel had not been briefed.

First the tiny creature sailed right over the plastic collar that Harold had placed around the tree's trunk, called a "squirrel deflector." Then he shimmied down the branch and busied himself extracting the suet. She watched with rapt fascination as the creature tugged and gnawed. She rapped hard on the glass. He paused and looked up at her, but seemed unconcerned. She found herself smiling, secretly cheering him on. Finally he gained access, bit off a huge chunk of fat, and scurried back down the limb.

Outside, her neighbor, Pat Walsh, steered his John Deere tractor toward the copse of maple trees that grew along the upper portion of his property. It was sugaring time. Each tree would be tapped with a small metal spout, and a metal bucket hung to help catch the sap. The warmer the weather, the faster the pails would fill. More efficient farmers had switched over to the plastic hosing that now wound its way through neighboring farms like industrial webbing. But Pat was a man of tradition. He also continued to sugar the old-fashioned way, stoking his fire twenty-four hours a day until all the water had been boiled away, leaving a vat of golden sweet liquid. For days the surrounding countryside would be filled with white smoke carrying the sweet smell of butter, wood, and maple sugar on the wind.

She waited until Pat wove his way into the thick woods before settling into one of the wicker chairs. Sunlight warmed her face. She closed her eyes as though she might somehow drink it in.

In the short time she had lived in Dorsetville, she had come to love the country, a fact that still puzzled her friends back in Queens.

"What do people do up there in the wilderness besides watch the grass grow?" Anything past the Throggs Neck Bridge was considered wilderness by her friends.

"You'll be bored to tears in no time," some predicted.

But they had been wrong. She liked living in the country. She liked the feel of Dorsetville. She even liked the quirky characters that frequented the Country Kettle, which often surprised her. She wasn't long on patience, and some of the folks around here could try your nerves. For instance, every one of them could quote the menu item for item, yet they had to look it over every time they came in as though seeing it for the very first time.

But regardless of their laid-back pace, and the tendency of shopkeepers to want to chat instead of selling you their wares, or the fact that Charlie Littman, the mailman, had a better handle on the magazines she subscribed to than she did, Wendy had grown to love the town. Through some alchemy, for the first time in her life she felt a real kinship with a place. Dorsetville had become home.

She had arrived in Dorsetville via an ad that John Moran had placed in the *New York Times* out of sheer desperation. The ad cost him $500 a clip to run. But the house had been on the market for over three years. It was an estate sale, and the heirs called religiously every week to inquire why it hadn't sold. As soon as Wendy spied it she made the two-and-a-half-hour drive from the city to see it the same day.

It didn't take more than a quick glance to understand why the property was being sold dirt cheap. The yard was overrun with briars; large sections of the stone fence encircling the property had fallen over; trees toppled in winter storms were strewn everywhere. One large tree had taken out an upstairs window and half the chimney.

Inside had fared no better. Mice scurried inside walls; the kitchen, circa 1950, had enough red Formica countertops and yellow linoleum to make her feel as though she had walked into McDonald's, and the rest of the floors looked as though they hadn't been cleaned in half a century.

Everywhere plaster was cracked or decaying. Ceilings were even worse. In several places the plaster had completely crumbled, leaving an underbelly of thin wooden strips exposed. And when Harold got his first look, he emerged from the basement shaking his head. The home's primary heat source was an old coal furnace.

Harold did his best to dissuade her, but Wendy saw through the flaws. She saw possibilities. Instead of flaking plaster, there would be soft, buttery yellow painted walls; a fire would hiss and crackle in the living room's stone fireplace, its light reflecting off the chestnut woodwork and doors now darkened with age. And once the floors had been resanded and tiled, she would fill the house with hand-hooked rugs and overstuffed furniture, and hang chintz curtains everywhere.

But mostly she had been attracted to the house by the quiet peace that stole through every room. Later, when she learned the previous owner had been a woman of great prayer, she knew that the peace had come from her faith in God's earnest love, and somehow that peace had been embedded in the home along with the plaster and the wood. Perhaps it would act as a healing balm to her troubled marriage, the very reason she had decided to move out of the city.

For months, she and Harold had painted and sanded, working feverishly to restore the house, until their knuckles bled and their backs ached. But during that entire time, neither had spoken of Harold's infidelity. The move—this house—was a new beginning. The past was the past. Both became adept at acting as though it had never happened. But all the while she worried that it might happen again, and now it had.

Wendy stared into the depths of her coffee mug as a fortune-teller might search for hidden truth among the tea leaves.

For weeks, she had tried to ignore the signs, but lately it had become only too clear. Unexplained absences. Stories that didn't quite line up. She was certain that Harold was having another affair.

She nervously twisted her long red hair while wondering who she was more angry with—herself or Harold. She should throw him out on his ear and be done with him for good. That lying, cheating rat. How could he do this to her again after he had promised? But she couldn't. Why? Because she still loved him. Talk about lame.

Maybe it was his dark, swarthy good looks, or his thick, muscular chest. All she knew was that when he walked into a room smelling of sweat and Lifebuoy soap, her knees went weak. And when he smiled that crooked boyish grin, she felt a heat rising, a passion so intense that her mind would flood with images of ravishing his body like a heroine from some cheap romantic novel.

At times it gave her solace knowing that she wasn't the only woman Harold affected that way. Weekends, when the weather permitted, they would travel the countryside on his Harley-Davidson, an Ultra Classic Electric Glide with batwing fairing, cruise control, and a CD player that sounded better than most expensive home units. Harold had spared no expense on this toy. It was quite an attention-getter. Park it anywhere and men were attracted like bees to honey. Women also sauntered over—only it was Harold, not the bike, that was the focus of their attention.

Last summer she had almost come to blows with some young blonde sporting a bare midriff and a sassy smile who had the nerve to slip her phone number into Harold's pants pocket when she thought Wendy wasn't looking.

Her coffee was growing cold, yet she couldn't summon the energy to get up and reheat it. She grabbed the new *Family Circle* magazine, with a note from Charlie Littman that her subscription was about to run out. Only in Dorsetville. She placed it on the skirted table and set the mug on top.

From the backwoods, a small family of deer gathered by the stone wall. Pat had finished setting out the pails and was headed back toward the barn. The buck watched him disappear before giving the signal, a flick of his tail. His retinue gathered close to his heels and together they sallied over the wall, heading toward the small stream that ran along the length of the property.

The deer made her think of Harold—the born-and-raised city boy who had reluctantly moved to the country. He had turned into a wide-eyed kid. Every animal sighting was treated as a major event. His enthusiasm always made her laugh. During hunting season, he had put out dozens of salt licks, hoping to entice the deer to safety.

"Just let a hunter step a foot on my property and and I'll run them down with my truck," he said, meaning it.

No wonder she loved him. What woman wouldn't? He was strong, handsome, sweet, funny, and incredibly sexy. But did she love him enough to forgive him . . . *again*? The old adage rang through her mind. *Once, shame on you. Twice, shame on me.*

She pulled a crocheted afghan over her legs, a find from last year's church tag sale. Maybe she just wasn't meant to be happily married. Harold was husband number three.

Her first husband had left her $20,000 in credit card debt, borrowed to feed his gambling habit. It had taken her three years of working double shifts to pay it off.

She met husband number two on a Waldbaum's checkout line. She would later suspect that his proposal of marriage had little to do with love. She was just another food source. When they met, he weighed just less than two hundred pounds, which she would later learn was the result of a ten-week crash diet.

They purchased a small duplex a block and a half down from his parents' place, which made it convenient for her four-hundred-pound mother-in-law to deliver the baked goods she purchased in bulk from the Freihofer's outlet store over in Flushing. Within a few weeks, the true identity of the man she had married began—literally—to emerge.

Evenings, they would sit home and Wendy would watch him graze his way through boxes of *babka* and chocolate cakes, pecan coffee rolls, and chocolate cookies. Since his idea of exercise was never more than soaking his feet in an inflatable kiddy pool stationed in the backyard while listening to the baseball games on the radio, he eventually ballooned to 384 pounds. Romance was quickly lost in the rolls of flab.

The marriage lasted less than a year. The divorce papers for number two arrived on her thirty-fifth birthday.

Then she met Harold, who was handsome, athletic, and had no strong propensity toward food or gambling other than playing the weekly lottery, and even though she had sworn never to marry again, they had run off to Vegas within the first week of meeting. They were married in one of the ubiquitous wedding chapels along the strip by a man who looked and spoke like Tim Conway. They had been married five years when she discovered the affair, which had been going on for several months before she had finally gotten suspicious. This time she was smarter.

Harold knew she worked the late shift on Thursdays so he would never suspect that when he left work this evening, she would be tailing him in a rented car she planned to pick up this morning over at Avis in Waterbury. If Harold was having an affair, she meant to find out with whom.

It was 8 A.M. when Mayor Roger Martin stepped through Sheriff Bromley's office door, and he was braced for a fight. He had come to deliver the news that due to another round of budget cuts, the sheriff would have to let one of his deputies go.

The mayor stood in front of the sheriff's desk and hemmed and hawed, then paced back and forth as he explained in detail the state of the town's dwindling budget, and how each department must do its share to keep the town from going into debt, all the while fully expecting a torrent of swearing and name-calling that would have his ears ringing for days. But much to his surprise, the sheriff took the news without comment. He even joked about buying the mayor breakfast at the Country Kettle since things at City Hall were so tight. Mayor Martin left the sheriff's office baffled.

What the mayor didn't know was that the sheriff could hardly contain his joy. Since Hill was the last man hired, he would logically be the first man to go. That's how the system worked, and there was absolutely nothing the union could do about it. No more crashed vehicles. No more complaints. No more need for economy-size bottles of antacids. Oh happy day!

But this state of euphoria was short-lived when, the very next day, Deputy Ed Hinman handed in his resignation.

"I hate to leave the force," Ed told him, "but the software company where my wife works is moving to California, and they've offered her a hefty raise and a promotion if she moves out there. It's just too good a deal for us to pass up."

Bromley said he understood and wished him the best, fighting back the bitter taste of disappointment. Looked like Hill was staying.

At two o'clock, Deputy Neal Green, who had worked on the force for nearly thirty years, walked in and said he was retiring. "Vicky's just retired from the post office and we want to start traveling before we're too old and decrepit to move."

Bromley said he understood and wished him the best. He waited until Green was safely out the door before giving in to a full-scale attack of depression.

With both officers resigning, Hill was now the senior officer—which meant that Hill would be with him until the day he died or retired. The sheriff moaned, put his head in his hands, and wondered if it was too late to start again someplace else, anywhere away from Hill.

Betty knocked lightly on the door and stepped in. Harley, the sheriff's one-hundred-pound German shepherd, lifted his head slightly, then went back to sleep. The sheriff reached for his bottle of Tums.

"You okay?" Betty asked, handing him a pink message slip. "You look a little pale."

"Indigestion. What's this?"

"The highway department called. They want to remind you

that the governor's motorcade will need an escort through the construction site along Route 7 tomorrow morning. They're widening the road."

"Have Neal or Ed take care of this." He handed her the slip back.

"I can't."

"You can't?"

"They've both taken the rest of the week off."

"What?"

"They each have some sick time and accumulated personal days they want to use. What could I do? They're leaving in a few weeks," she explained, taking a step back. The sheriff's face had turned an angry red.

"They can't both take off!" he shouted.

Harley got up and slid underneath a side table.

She took another step back. "Well . . . actually . . . according to union rules . . . they can."

"Can this day get any better?" he swore. "So that leaves us with . . ."

"Hill." She moved out into the hall.

He put his face into his hands. "If I send him, that means he'll have to drive a cruiser."

"I'm afraid so. Unless you want him to hitch a ride with the highway crew."

"Can we do that?" he asked hopefully.

"I doubt it," she said. "Besides, he'll need the cruiser in case of trouble."

"Don't even think it," he warned her.

"It's just that with Hill . . . well . . . you never know."

"Why does God hate me?"

If the sheriff hadn't promised to transport a prisoner from

Manchester down to Chester, he'd escort the governor himself, but it was too late to make other arrangements.

"Hill!" he bellowed. Hill came running. "I have something I need you to do for me tomorrow," he began.

"Anything, Chief."

Betty handed Hill the memo, then sped back to her desk.

"The governor's motorcade is passing that highway construction site out on Route 7 around eleven o'clock," he explained. "I need you to cover it. Think you could do that without screwing anything up?"

"A piece of cake, Chief."

"Seems like I've heard that before."

"I'll need the cruiser," Hill said tentatively.

"Yeah, I know," Bromley said, going back to his paperwork. *"Betty!"* he hollered down the hall.

"Yes, Sheriff," she hollered back. No one used the intercom in this office.

"Give Hill the spare set of keys to the cruiser."

"Yes sir."

"And . . . Hill?" the sheriff said.

Hill turned expectantly. "Yes, Sheriff?"

"If anything happens to that vehicle, you'd better pray that you're in a body cast. It's the only thing that will keep me from killing you. You got that?"

"Yes, Chief."

"And don't call me 'Chief'!"

Chapter Fifteen

"Hi, *Mr. Metcalf.* It's me . . . Gracie, down at the station. I just got word that the governor's motorcade is passing through Route 7 around noon. Lucky for me that I happened to stop at the Country Kettle and overheard Sheriff Bromley telling the highway crew chief all about it.

"Did you know that those men have coffee between eight and eight-fifteen every morning? I thought you might want to know that in case you ever need to track them down. You know, for a segment or something.

"Anyway, I overheard the sheriff telling the men about the motorcade and that he was sending Deputy Hill along to direct traffic.

"What did they say about that? They seemed a little shocked.

"Did you know that they're widening Route 7 along that stretch of highway by Nelson's farm? Neither did I. I really have to get out more. But it's so hard, when you're working full-time *and* raising a family.

"Did I tell you that my little Davie made the Dorsetville T-ball team? I didn't? Well, you should see my little tyke dressed in his uniform. He's sweeter than spun sugar.

"What was I saying about the governor's motorcade? Oh yes. I thought you might want to film it for tonight's *Around the Town* segment. Of course, you won't be able to see his face behind that dark glass, but that doesn't matter.

"Wouldn't it be great if he decided to pay a visit, here in Dorsetville? I wonder if the mayor knows he's passing through. He's coming around lunchtime. Maybe he could invite the governor over to the Country Kettle.

"Today's special is Brunswick stew, and I'm sure the governor would love to sample one of Lori's desserts afterward, aren't you?

"Have you tried her new amaretto sponge cake? It's to die for. I was just saying to Betty Olsen the other day . . ."

Yep . . . things couldn't be going better, Hill thought, leaning against the police cruiser's freshly polished leather seats and savoring the feel of being behind the wheel again. He ran his right hand over the steering wheel and vowed that nothing was going to happen to send him back pounding the pavement ever again.

He cruised along Meadow Street and spied postman Charlie Littman, bundled in layers of protective clothing, on Doc Hammon's front porch. The temperature had started to plummet again. Charlie's thick, gloved hands were sorting through a bunch of letters as Hill passed by. He beeped the horn and waved. Charlie stared back, openmouthed.

Hill took a right-hand turn and headed down the lane that wound its way along the river and past Mill's Hotel and Conference Center. He heard that the owner, Barry Hornibrook, was building a boathouse and planned to rent motorboats this summer to his guests. It would also house the new cabin cruiser he had just bought to replace the one that he had lost a few months back. The Gallagher twins had blown it up.

His stomach began to growl. He was getting hungry. It had been hours since he'd had a bite to eat. He had gotten up early this morning and sped over to the department's garage, making certain that the cruiser had a full tank of gas and that all the equipment was in tip-top shape. As self-improvement guru Rich Malone said, *"Always remember that God is in the details."*

Hill was on the final segment of the course. It had changed his life forever. Who would have known that the secret to success lay in simply taking control of one's thoughts? But it was true. In fact, he saw today's assignment as a prime example.

For weeks he had visualized himself back behind the wheel of the cruiser, patrolling the countryside, and here he was. Amazing! Now he was working hard on his next plan, to become a detective, although he hadn't a clue what he would "detect," since there were no robberies, murders, rapes, break-ins, or other serious crimes taking place in Dorsetville; but he figured he had time to work all that out. He had plenty of time. He had to make sergeant first. But he wasn't worried. If things kept going the way they had been, it would be a piece of cake.

His stomach rumbled again. He should get himself a little something to eat before heading out of town. Lori Peterson's cinnamon buns came to mind—light as a cumulus cloud and drizzled with white icing. If he closed his eyes, he could even smell them. His stomach gave another little lurch. That cinched it. He looked at his watch. He had another thirty minutes before he needed to meet the town crew, so he headed in the direction of the Country Kettle, looping around Main Street.

Regardless of the fact that he was weak from hunger, he focused on his official duties, deliberately easing off the gas, studying each shop with a trained eye as he looked for irregularities.

Just because there wasn't any crime in Dorsetville (unless you counted Pete Johnson's temporary theft of a bag of rock salt last winter: he had been engaged in a heated conversation with someone on the town crew about the mess of the roads up where he lived and walked right out to his truck without paying—but he did come back a few hours later to settle up with Mark Stone), that didn't mean that he could just sit on his laurels and let things slide. Nope, he had a sworn duty to protect the citizens of this fair town.

The cruiser's highly polished surface reflected off the glass window of the smoke shop. Mildred Dunlop was just parking her car out in front. Today was Thursday, which meant the weekly edition of *Crosswords and Brain Teasers* had arrived. Mildred hadn't missed an issue in thirty years.

A few doors down, Jonathan Kelly was sweeping the sidewalk in front of his bar and grill. Tonight was poker night. He wanted to get his chores done earlier so he could set up the back room. He was especially eager today to get things in order so he could concentrate on how he was going to win back that twenty dollars he had lost to Sam Rosenberg last week.

A large produce truck was pulling into Dinova's rear parking lot. Hill parked the cruiser and went to inspect the emission sticker on the cab of the truck. Hill felt it important to let deliverymen know that inspection violations would not be tolerated in Dorsetville. Citizens had a right to clean air.

Everything checked out, so he got back into the car and settled once more behind the wheel. He had just backed out of the parking space when he remembered: he hadn't tested the cruiser's lights or sirens. What if he needed them? What if the governor needed to be rushed through town, or if a call came in about a bank holdup? That was unlikely, but he could hope.

He flicked on the switch. The red-and-yellow lights bounced off the storefronts. The siren's loud, piercing blare made windowpanes shake, and Reverend Curtis, who had been walking his dog, felt nearly faint from fright.

George walked into the church, his work boots leaving flakes of dried mud in his wake, feeling like a new man. His license had been restored, and his van was parked outside.

Sirius Faithwait had been here earlier finishing the masonry work in Saint Anthony's niche. George headed over in hopes that the mortar was drying quickly. With any luck, the saint might be back in place by tomorrow.

George ran a light hand over the damp cement. Sirius had done a good job, nice and smooth. He stepped back and nodded with satisfaction. Yep, no one could tell that it wasn't the original stonework.

He bent down, searching for his chisel. He had loaned it to the mason, who had promised to leave it right here. George was repairing a shower leak over at the Petersons' this afternoon and had to remove a row of tiles. He'd told Sirius to leave it right here, next to the candle stand, but it was nowhere in sight. Maybe it rolled somewhere. He bent down and made a search along the perimeter. Nope, it wasn't there either. Darn it. He needed that tool! That's what he got for being so good-natured.

Well, maybe Sirius put it in the storage closet. He walked over to the far side of the church, lifted up the potted palm, and grabbed the key. He unlocked the door and threw on the light, but nothing happened. He jiggled the switch. Still nothing. Must be a bulb, he figured.

He didn't feel like tramping all the way out to his van for a flashlight and then coming all the way back. He got enough exercise lifting tools and fixtures all day. So he reached inside his shirt pocket for a book of matches. A cigar stub tumbled out onto the floor. George dusted it off and stuffed it back in his pocket.

He struck the match against the door's wood frame. The small orb of light did little to dispel the thick darkness inside the windowless storage area. He lifted the flame high over the assortment of boxes, hymnals, old bulletins, and dried flowers. The place was a fire trap. If he had had his summons book, he would have written it up. Just because he was a parishioner didn't mean he could let things like this go.

The matches burned quickly, and he lit a succession, wading his way deeper and deeper into the closet.

"Gosh darn it!" he bellowed, skinning his shins against a prie-dieu.

Where was that tool anyway? Hey, wait a minute. Where was Saint Anthony's statue? He and Ted had put it right there in the center of the closet. Now it was gone.

Well, if that didn't beat all! After taking all those precautions to make sure it didn't get damaged, some dang fool had moved it!

"George? You in there?" Mrs. Norris called from outside the door.

"Yeah, I'm here. Ouch!"

"What happened?"

"Burnt my fingers with a match."

"What in heaven's name are you doing there in the dark?"

"I'm looking for my chisel," he said.

"You mean this?" she asked.

"Where did you find that?"

"It was right here on this box of old hymnals. Now come out of there. I need you in the rectory. The kitchen sink has just backed up and there's water everywhere."

Chapter Sixteen

❦

*B*y *eleven o'clock,* a squall sealed in a forty-mile radius with a white curtain of snow. Visibility was reduced to just a few inches, and the temperature plummeted. People went in search of snow shovels and wondered when winter would ever end.

Those traversing the snow-encrusted roads began to question (as many local folks are wont to do during the month of March) what exactly it was about New England winters that they enjoyed. As they scraped car windshields and sanded icy walks, their minds were wistfully drawn to warmer climates. The Tribury Travel Agency in Woodstock would receive a record number of inquiries this morning on Bermuda cruises and Florida getaways.

Triple-A also garnered its fair share of calls, with a mixture of car problems—dead batteries, doors iced shut, and the usual assortment of vehicles that had slid off the road. Motorists' tempers flared, their moods growing as dark as the storm clouds that had taken the countryside by siege.

But Father James had awakened with praise bubbling from his lips. Maybe it had something to do with the good news that Doc Hammon was coming home the day after tomorrow and that Father Dennis was returning next week. He had missed them both and would be happy as a pig in mud to have them back.

Father James could barely wait to see the look on Doc's face when he discovered that Dexter was slowly coming out of his coma. Although no one knew just how much brain damage the child might have incurred, there were hopeful signs.

He also knew that Doc would be pleased as punch to know that Arlene had finally consented to place Fred in Glen Oaks, and even though it had been a difficult adjustment, the tired look in her eyes had seemingly disappeared overnight and the apple-red blush had returned to her cheeks.

"Shouldn't we be traveling a mite slower, considering the weather conditions?" Arlene asked, gripping hold of the dashboard for dear life.

This morning's rain had turned to sleet, and she feared that if Father James didn't slow down, they'd never make it to visit Fred in one piece.

"Heavenly hosts surround us," he said, making light of her concerns.

"All of whom I suspect are on Prozac," she said with a nervous little laugh.

"All right. I get the message. Now go on with your story."

"Now, where was I? Oh yes, I was telling you that I wondered if finding my grandmother Hattie's tea set was a sign that she was still watching over me."

Father James flicked on the blinker. "The Bible tells us that 'we are surrounded by a cloud of witnesses, cheering us on.' I'm sure that includes your grandmother."

"I think so too," Arlene agreed, leaning forward. "What's that up ahead?"

Traffic had come to a standstill.

"Looks like a truck has flipped over," he said.

"Oh dear, I wonder if anyone is hurt."

He released his seat belt, grabbed the small black case in the backseat containing a vial of consecrated oil, and jumped outside.

"You stay here," he told her. "I'm going to see if anyone needs my services."

He wound his way through the line of cars up ahead, whose drivers gathered to discuss the accident. A car was pinned beneath the tractor trailer.

"You think anyone is trapped inside?" asked a man in a three-piece wool suit.

"The ambulance arrived a few minutes ago," said a woman holding a small child. "I saw them take out a stretcher."

The area around the accident had been cordoned off by the state police. Father James hailed a state trooper and asked for permission to enter the area.

He unzipped his jacket, revealing his white collar. "I thought someone might need my services."

The officer let him pass through.

"Over here, Father!" Ben waved. The station's video camera rested on his shoulder and a press badge hung from his neck. Off to one side stood Timothy and Sam.

"What happened?" Father James asked, surveying the wreckage up close.

"You wouldn't believe it if I told you," Ben said. "Deputy Hill saved the governor's life."

"Hill what?" Father James couldn't have heard that correctly.

"As you're always saying, Father James, God moves in mysterious ways," Sam reminded him.

"That's his cruiser underneath the truck," Timothy offered.

"Is Frank all right?"

"A sprained wrist," Sam answered. "That's him over there lying on the stretcher."

Except for his arm in a sling, Hill looked fine. In fact, he was having an animated conversation with a reporter from channel 8.

"You should have seen it, Father," Timothy said. "Hill bailed out of the cruiser just before it crashed."

"That's how he hurt his wrist," Sam explained.

"It sure was something to see," Timothy continued.

"Just like an action movie," Ben added, his voice charged with excitement. "You should have seen it. This truck lost control on the ice and was barreling down the highway, heading straight for the governor's limousine . . ."

"Then it started to skid," Sam chimed in.

"And Deputy Hill drives the cruiser right into the side of the truck, seconds before it rams into the governor's car," Ben concluded.

"Amazing!" Father James said.

"And we have the whole thing on tape," Ben said proudly. "That reporter from channel 8 has offered us five hundred dollars to let him use it on tonight's news."

"Well, I've had enough excitement for one day," Sam said,

tightening up the collar of his coat. "Besides, I'm freezing. Anyone else coming?"

"Can you drop Ben and me back at the station? We have some editing to do before airtime," Timothy said, his face bright with excitement.

"Maybe we can stop at the high school and pick up Matthew," added Ben, who was thinking about the last time they had tried to edit on their own.

"Oh, yeah . . ."

"Sheriff, there's a call for you on line one," Betty hollered down the hall.

"Who is it?" he bellowed.

"Some reporter from a news station."

"Sheriff Bromely here," he said, picking up the receiver. "What can I do for you?"

"Sheriff, this is Don Akins. I'm a reporter with channel 8. Our mobile crew just returned from a crash site on Route 7 and I wanted to get your comments."

"Crash site?" He started to get that familiar sinking feeling in the pit of his stomach.

"A truck just totaled a police cruiser. It says here in my notes that the driver of the cruiser was a Deputy Hill."

Deputy Hill stepped into his apartment and playfully kicked the door shut with his foot. He had left this apartment several hours ago a mere man. He had returned a hero. The foreman said he was nominating him for a medal of honor. Hot dog! This called for a celebration, he thought, heading into the kitchen to fix himself a root beer float.

He opened the freezer compartment and pulled out a half-eaten quart of Breyers vanilla ice cream and looked at it with distress. How was he supposed to scoop it out of the container with a sprained right hand? He put it back in the freezer and went to lie down. There was only so much excitement a guy could take.

Just before he drifted off to sleep, a thought came to him like a note slipped under the door. Hero or not, how was he going to explain to Sheriff Bromley that he had totaled another cruiser? And how had he managed to get himself into this jam again, especially since he had worked so hard at preventing it?

Hill had arrived a full thirty minutes before the motorcade was due and carefully parked the cruiser a safe distance away from all the construction work. There were men with dump trucks and backhoes, riveting guns and gravel trucks. There was no way he was going to let anything happen to the chief's cruiser, and as an added precaution, he placed several orange cones around the car before heading to the site.

Meanwhile, Ben Metcalf, Timothy McGee, and Sam Rosenberg had arrived and were setting up the camera off to the side of the road. Their plan was to shoot the governor's motorcade as it flew past and incorporate it into this week's *Around the Town* segment.

Within the hour, the roads began icing up. Traffic had slowed to a crawl. The crew chief walked over to Hill, who had just pulled down the earflaps of his hat, to ask his advice.

"What do you think? Should we call it quits? The roads are getting pretty slippery. I'd hate to have a car spin out of control and plow into one of my guys. The highway department over in Manchester lost one of their men that way."

Hill was inordinately pleased to be sought out for his opinion. He leaned back on his heels and took a great deal of time inspecting the skies, now gunmetal gray.

"I'd wrap it up and go home," Hill said sagely.

The chief turned and told his foreman, "Tell the men to pack it up. Move the heavy equipment off to the side of the road and out of harm's way. Can you move the cruiser, Deputy? We'll need to park the Payloader over there."

There weren't many times in his life that Deputy Hill felt a part of a team, but he did this morning, and was eager to join the group effort. Freezing rain had coated the road in a thin cover of ice, and he slid his way across the road en route to the car. Once the crews had restationed all of their equipment, he figured that he'd park and wait for the governor's limo to pass, then head back to town.

He moved the cruiser partly into the road, then stopped. The wiper blades were useless against the ice-encrusted windshield. He threw the car into park, grabbed the scraper from off the backseat, and hopped out. Meanwhile, the Payloader pulled up behind him and the driver jumped out.

"See you in town," he shouted, racing across the road to his car.

It was then that Hill spied the headlights traveling from the east. The way they were configured, he knew that the governor's motorcade was advancing some twenty minutes earlier than scheduled.

Darn! Now what was he supposed to do? Leave the cruiser sticking out on the side of the road and chance having it sideswiped, or move it? Meanwhile, the governor's limo was edging closer. He could see a faint outline of the state and national flags waving in the breeze.

His mind went into fast-forward. If he took the time to

move the cruiser, he might miss directing the motorcade through the work zone. Granted, no one was working. Most everyone had left to go home. But still, Sheriff Bromley had promised the governor that an officer would be stationed there to see him through. This was his first serious assignment in months, and he could feel himself blowing it.

His mind was racing, spewing out thoughts like loose lug nuts off a radial tire. He was about to come undone. Finally he made a decision. The cruiser had to be moved. He hopped back in the car, threw it into drive, and heard the sound of a heavy vehicle heading his way. He rolled down his driver's side window and gasped.

A large truck, with horn blaring, was barreling down the hill from the west, and the cruiser was right in its path. He figured that with the current road conditions, the driver had a better chance of sledding in the tropics than of stopping that rig.

"If anything happens to that vehicle, you'd better pray that you're in a body cast. It's the only thing that will keep me from killing you," the sheriff had said.

For a fleeting moment, he considered throwing himself in front of the truck and having it done with. It looked as though his life was over anyway. Meanwhile, in the distance, the governor's limo was sailing forward completely unaware of the danger that lay just up ahead.

Later, folks would say that Hill displayed rare courage in attempting to save the governor's life. But in reality, he had just wanted to save the cruiser and his career. A small patch of open field lay directly across the highway. He hit the gas, sending the cruiser shooting across the highway like a hockey puck.

At that moment, the limo driver, who had been thinking about his hot date with a Sears catalog model that evening and not the road, finally awoke to what was happening up ahead and yelled to the governor, "Hold on!"

Meanwhile, the truck, which was hauling several hundred cases of Pepsi, Diet Pepsi, and Mountain Dew, had begun to fishtail. Hill eyeballed the charging mass of steel but figured there was just enough room between them to get the cruiser to safety. Unfortunately, he had failed high school physics not once but twice, and had forgotten to factor in the mass-times-speed ratio. The weight of those cases of soda was driving the rig faster than he anticipated.

Hill was halfway across the road when the cruiser hit the truck's side panel with enough force to shake his fillings loose. The impact sent the truck into a tailspin, taking the cruiser along with it. He heard the now-familiar crunch of metal, saw the hood begin to bend like a piece of tinfoil, and did the only thing he could—he bailed out.

After that, things got a little blurry. He was lying on the ground, his wrist hurt, and the world was spinning. When he finally sat up, he saw the blue-and-white squad car sandwiched between ten tons of metal and steel like a piece of deli ham.

"Oh no," he moaned.

Miraculously, there was a bright side. The cruiser had forced the truck to the other side of the road, thus saving the governor's car.

Soon folks were rushing over, telling him that they had never seen anything quite so brave. The governor pushed through the crowd, looped an arm around his shoulder, and told everyone that he was a hero.

"I'm going to make a personal call to your boss and recommend a promotion. How does 'sergeant' sound, Deputy?" the governor asked, patting him on the back.

He remembered thinking on the ride back into town, Who knows? Maybe I might not need a body cast for protection after all.

After Father James had made certain that his services were no longer needed at the crash sight, and had dropped Arlene off at the nursing home, he headed straight over to Mercy Hospital.

The ride took under twenty minutes. Processing Hill as a hero might take him a mite longer. As he pulled into the parking space labeled *Reserved for Clergy,* he concluded that life was surely filled with surprises.

The warmth of the hospital felt good after standing outside in the cold for so long. He probably should have listened to Mrs. Norris and worn his woolen socks. But he had ignored her suggestion, like a rebellious youngster. A priest should allow a housekeeper to direct his life only so far, right?

As he waited for the elevator, two giggling young candy-stripers laughed and joked their way down the hall. Their joyous sound, like wind chimes, lifted his spirits. Seconds later, as he was whisked to the top floor, he reflected on the sound of their laughter. It was a gift from God, sorely underused by adults. Children's laugher came unbidden. Adults, however, often felt as though it must be rationed like food stamps.

He was just formulating a wonderful sermon about the benefit of laughter when the doors slid open and he was greeted by Mike Gallagher, grinning like a child at Christmas.

"The doctors say that Dexter is coming out of the coma."

Dexter heard his father's voice. It seemed to be coming from the bright orb of light on the other side of the meadow.

"The doctors told us not to get too excited, but we feel confident that he's coming out of it."

Wildflowers grew profusely along the pathway that wound its way toward the light. He paused to pick a small bouquet. His mother liked flowers. He missed her. It seemed as though he had been gone forever.

The light was growing stronger, drawing him near.

"I told God that if he brought my brother back, I'd be a priest."

That was Rodney's voice. Become a priest? Was he crazy?

Dexter broke out into a run.

Chapter Seventeen

*T*he last shards of light backlit the woods surrounding the middle-class neighborhood. Wendy sat parked in the rented Honda Civic several doors down from a small white cottage owned by a Ms. Marsha Littleford, at 32 Sky View Terrace.

She killed the engine and doubled-checked the camera. Dusk had begun to settle in, but there was still enough light to get a clear shot of Harold as he went to visit his newest mistress. She wanted no mistake when she hired a divorce lawyer. She wanted proof that he was cheating, *again*.

Without taking her eyes off the house, she rummaged through her purse in search of her Virginia Slims, feeling anger hot and seething. How dare he do this to her again!

It hadn't been hard to validate her suspicions. She found the evidence needed in Harold's sock drawers—canceled checks made out to Marsha Littleford. She had to give the woman credit. At least she had made him pay for it.

Did he really believe that she would not find out? *My God, the idiot had written the woman checks, and then hid them in his sock drawer!* . . . It was as if he wanted to be caught.

What about all of those promises Harold had made? It would never happen again, he had said. It had been a meaningless fling. All he ever *really* wanted was to be with Wendy. The lying scum!

She pushed in the cigarette lighter, waited to hear it pop, and lit up, ignoring the sign posed just above the radio, *This is a smoke-free automobile*. She took a couple of drags, cranked down the window a hair, and let the wind catch the smoke, pulling it along like the tail of a kite.

How had their marriage gotten derailed? Was it something she had said, or done, or failed to do? Had she been too preoccupied with Harvest and her problems and not cognizant enough of Harold's needs? But what needs? A can of beer, Monday night football, and an occasional roll in the hay during half-time. Maybe that was it. Their marriage lacked romance.

What puzzled her most was that, lately, it seemed as though their marriage had never been better. They went on day trips. They had even spent a memorable weekend at Foxwoods Casino. She had won $2,500 at the slots, which she used to buy them matching suede coats.

The fact that their wedding anniversary was only a week away really burned her bloomers. They had talked about taking a cruise. You'd think that he would have timed things a little better. Luckily she hadn't bought tickets.

Harold's truck rounded the corner. Wendy stubbed out the

cigarette and reached for the camera. Within seconds, she had caught Harold in the zoom lens. She was pleased to see him wearing his hangdog expression, the one she knew well. It meant he had had a hard day at the plant. If he had been wearing his Cheshire cat smile she might have jumped out and pummeled him to the ground. Somehow it was comforting to note that his new mistress received the same kind of greeting as she did.

She snapped several photos in rapid succession. Harold getting out of the truck. Harold walking down the brick walk. Harold waiting at the front door. Harold being ushered inside the house.

The snake!

She lit another cigarette and puffed away like a steam engine.

Suspecting one's husband of having an affair and actually witnessing it were two entirely different things. Right now, her cigarette wasn't the only thing that was smoking.

She had gotten a slight glimpse of Marsha Littleford as she had opened the front door. (And how brazen was that? You'd think if a woman was stealing someone's husband, she'd have the decency to make him use the back door.)

Ms. Littleford was moderately attractive, a little worn around the edges, and certainly no knockout. So what was the draw? What did she have that Wendy didn't?

Curiosity finally got the better of her. She locked the car and headed out for a closer peak.

The street of older homes remained dark in the pre-evening light. Most folks were still at work or on their way home. There was no one around to notice a tall, red-haired woman wearing white rubber-soled shoes casing number 32.

The front of the house was dark, but light was reflected off the back lawn. She quietly made her way toward the rear of the property. The muffled strains of a soft Latin beat were coming from the glass sliders. Hugging the house, she edged closer until she had a clear view.

"Why that no-good, cheating . . ."

The room was generously lit and provided a bird's-eye view of her husband in the arms of Ms. Littleford. They were dancing.

"Ouch!" the woman complained. "You keep stepping on my toes."

"Sorry," Harold apologized. "I'll get it right this time."

Well, if that didn't take the cake. Not only was Harold cheating on her, he was dancing the rumba.

"Al, would you please lift your feet?" Barbara Bromley yelled over the sound of her Kenmore PowerMate.

The sheriff's German shepherd had managed to spread enough loose hair on the living room carpet to make a nice-size winter coat, and her mah-jongg group was due in a few minutes.

The sheriff did as instructed. "I'm telling you, Barbara, I've had enough. I've made up my mind. I'm quitting, and don't try and talk me out of it."

"Don't you have some paperwork you can do back at your office?" She yanked a loose pillow out from behind her husband. Just as she suspected—a slew of dog hairs were hidden underneath.

"Haven't you heard a thing I've said this evening?" he growled.

"Yes, my dear, I heard. You're quitting as sheriff. You're tired of the constant aggravation and people butting into your affairs. They should leave you alone to run the department as you see fit. Does that about cover it? Al, get up. I have to vacuum the couch." She opened the cover to the vacuum and searched where the attachments were stored. The upholstery brush was missing.

The sheriff got up, swearing under his breath. "I don't know why I come home. Last week it was the quilters' group. The week before, some church committee. A man's house is supposed to be his castle, not Grand Central Station."

Barbara was still searching for the attachment. She had left it on top of the entertainment center. Al took it down and handed it to her.

"I'm telling you, Barbara, I won't be dictated to by the mayor or anyone else. Give Hill a promotion. Ha! For what? They want me to make him a sergeant! Now that's a laugh. Dogcatcher would be more likely."

Harley lifted his head and whined.

"Don't worry, boy, I wouldn't do that to you."

"It doesn't sound as though they're trying to run your department," she said, standing the cushions up against the couch to vacuum underneath. "The mayor was only making a suggestion, a suggestion that came down by way of the governor, I might add."

"Hum!"

"You can 'hum' all you want to, but the fact remains that Deputy Hill saved the governor's life, and probably several other innocent bystanders, by his action, and whether you like it or not, he's a hero and should be recognized as such."

"But they want me to make him a *sergeant*," he whined.

"So, make him a sergeant. Who's it going to hurt?" she said, turning off the vacuum.

"You can't be serious?"

"Then refuse the governor's request."

"Right—and effectively end my career. The mayor hinted that if I refused, he'd back my opponent come next election." He crashed back onto the couch. She just didn't get it.

The doorbell rang. Harley hurled himself against the front door, barking as if the legions of hell were demanding entrance.

Great, just what he needed. More women!

The sheriff threw on an old coat and headed outside into the brisk night air, his ears still ringing from the barrage of the women's questions.

"Is it really true? Did your deputy save the governor's life?"

"I heard that the civic group was having a ceremony in his honor. Do you know when, so I can plan to attend?"

"What about the rumor that he's being made a sergeant? Is that true, Sheriff?"

It was enough to make a teetolaling man want a drink.

He closed the door behind him and stepped out into the frigid night air. Would spring ever come? he wondered. It seemed as though the town had been under a deep freeze for months.

Harley had followed him outside and was busy sniffing the tires of Ethel's car. The fool women had lined the driveway with automobiles. Now he couldn't go back to the office if he wanted to, which he didn't.

The wind had picked up. He headed for his workshop, Harley close on his heels, nearly catching Harley's tail as he closed the shed door. The inside of the building seemed colder than it was outside. He switched on the overhead light and rushed over to turn the electric heater up full blast.

While he waited for the temperature to rise, he examined the ham radio sitting disassembled on his workbench. He had bought it over at the Woodbury flea market a few months back and had been working on it in his free time. Every time he looked at it, fond memories came flooding back. His dad had one just like it when he was a kid.

A lot of hours were spent hunched over that radio. It seemed so strange and mysterious back then to speak to people from other parts of the country, to hear their strange accents and exchange details about the weather or the kinds of fish that were running in their part of the woods. Later, his father had given him permission to run it on his own. Every day for months, he had rushed home after school, eager to scout the airwaves in search of friends his own age.

Finally, the chill was displaced by the steady flow of warm air. He unbuttoned his coat, casting it carelessly on a nearby sawhorse, and opened his toolbox in search of a small Phillips screwdriver. Harley threw himself down by his feet and placed his head on his paws, happy as a fox among chickens just to be with his master.

The sheriff slowly began to reconnect the web of wires, wondering if, when he was through, anyone would answer. Were there still ham radio operators out there, or had everyone switched over to the Internet?

He hoped they hadn't. He would need a hobby if he was turning in his badge.

Father James turned off the bedside lamp, feeling that it had been an extraordinary day. First, Deputy Hill had saved the governor, and then Dexter's neurologist had announced that the boy was slowly coming out of the coma.

"But I must caution you," he had warned the Gallaghers, "it's certain that he has suffered irreversible brain damage."

Lorraine remained undaunted and held steadfast to her belief that God would return her son whole.

She told Father James, "When Jesus returned the widow's child from the dead, he was fully restored, and since the Bible says that 'Jesus is the same yesterday, today, and forever,' I believe that same Lord is present now to restore my son to full health."

May it be as she believes, Father James prayed.

And while he had the Lord's ear, he figured he might as well say a special prayer for the Campbells. Arlene would need renewed strength as Fred's disease progressed, and Fred would need the tender care of those at Glen Oaks.

He prayed for the Petersons, who he heard were trying to adopt another child. He couldn't think of better parents. Their daughter, Sarah, was testimony to that.

For Wendy Davis, who had quietly sought his advice about her troubled marriage, and for her niece, Harvest, who he sensed had troubles of her own.

For Doc Hammon's recovery and the gift of many more years of good health.

He prayed for all the good people of Dorsetville who were privileged to call this wonderful little town their home. He doubted that there was a more caring, compassionate bunch of folks in all of New England. They worked hard to live the tenets of their faith.

And finally, he prayed for Father Dennis, who was due home shortly. He had missed his company, his laughter, and his eager enthusiasm for God's work. Father James also asked that God always make him mindful of the gifts his young priest brought to the parish, especially the gift of friendship.

He slipped down beneath the warm hand-sewn quilts piled on his bed and let his mind empty of all its thoughts, except one. This one he tucked underneath his pillow.

"Father James, I told God that if he let Dexter wake up, I'd be a priest," Rodney had told him, and it seemed as though God just might be taking him up on the offer.

The priest smiled. *Father Rodney . . .* it had a certain ring to it.

As the sleepy town hovered on the edge that separates the night skies from predawn light, the dreaming from the waking, a brown-robed hooded figure slipped unnoticed into Dexter's hospital room.

Jennie's voice wafted softly on the air.

See you later, Dexter. Tell my mother that I'll be waiting to meet her when she crosses over.

The light was blinding. He could no longer see the meadow. Something seemed to be pulling him through a tunnel.

"Dexter . . . it's time to return."

He took a deep breath and opened his eyes. Something was strange. The colors weren't as brilliant as in the meadow. Everything in the room seemed dull in contrast. Then he noticed the friar in a long brown robe standing over his bed.

"Welcome back, my child."

Dexter looked around the room. Hey! This wasn't his bedroom. There were machines and a white curtain and—cripes!—a needle was sticking out of his arm.

"Where am I? Let me go!" he demanded, staring at the plastic line pumping fluids into his body.

"You're in the hospital," the friar explained calmly. "Don't be alarmed. Everything is going to be all right now."

"Easy for you to say. You're not being used as a pin-cushion."

The friar laughed and reached out to gently touch the boy's cheek. As soon as his hand made contact, Dexter felt a wonderful sense of warmth spread from the top of his head to his toes. He grew sleepy. His eyes began to close.

Wait a minute! He was not going back to sleep until he got some answers. What was he doing here? He forced himself awake. But when he opened his eyes, the friar had vanished, and he was holding a bouquet of wildflowers that he had picked for his mother in the meadow.

The first pink rays of morning light filtered through the stained-glass windows that lined Saint Cecilia's sanctuary. All was quiet, and nothing stirred except the particles of dust that danced in the sunbeams gently caressing the oak pews.

The air was heavy with the scent of gardenias that Harriet had arranged around the altar. The friar breathed deeply. They reminded him of his boyhood.

Then his eyes came upon the crucifix. A peaceful smile played across his lips.

"Thank you, Lord, for allowing me the privilege of under-taking this wonderful mission. As you said, the people here in Dorsetville are good and faithful folks."

He thought of Arlene Campbell, the deep love she felt for her husband, and her willingness to sacrifice herself in order to keep a promise.

He thought about the Gallaghers, who had weathered one of life's most difficult trials, the near death of a child. Yet their faith had remained intact—and now, how that faith would become a testimony of hope for others!

He thought about Father James, a kind and caring priest, a true shepherd, and asked for God's special blessing upon this good man. "May he live a long and fruitful life."

And he smiled broadly when he thought about Frank Hill, who had come one night to ask for his intervention. It had been his pleasure to intercede on his behalf.

The friar bowed his head and prayed a special prayer that all those who had lost their faith might find their way to Dorsetville, where a special elixir of hope and charity could be found to soothe a troubled soul.

Then, lifting his arms in praise, he bestowed his own blessing upon this dear little town, and at the sound of his voice, there was the flutter of a thousand angels' wings.

When he was through praising God for his tender mercy and love, the friar rose and tightened the coarse rope around his waist before heading toward the altar. He stepped up to the lectern and removed a small parchment from his voluminous sleeve and placed it there.

Then, after paying homage to the sacred host inside the golden tabernacle, he made his way toward the supply closet and quietly closed the door.

Chapter Eighteen

G *eorge and Ted* arrived early at Saint Cecilia's, towing
a dolly. Its rubber wheels clicked and clacked along
the marble floors as they made their way toward the
supply closet. George had promised Father James that Saint
Anthony's statue would be back in place for the thanksgiving
mass being said for Dexter's miraculous recovery. Now, if
George could just find the statue.

"So where do you think we should look first?" Ted asked.

George cast an eye around the sanctuary. There weren't a
lot of places to hide a six-foot statue. "Beats me."

"Are you sure it's not in the closet?"

"I looked."

"Maybe I should look," Ted offered.

"Go ahead and look, but you won't find anything. I'm not blind."

Ted found the key and opened the locked supply-closet door.

"Light's out," George warned. "You're going to need a match to see anything in there."

Ted threw the switch. The closet was bathed in light.

"Well, if that don't beat all," George said, scratching his head. Both the light and the statue had been restored.

Wendy studied Harold's profile as he knelt praying, golden shards of light streaming through the church windows tinting his dark, curly locks in gold.

God, he is gorgeous, she thought, then chided herself. What's the matter with me? The man is a two-timing, lying womanizer. How could I possibly still be attracted to him?

I love him, that's how, she thought. So, what was she going to do?

She had told Father James about the affair when she had gone to him for advice.

"No marriage is perfect," he had counseled. "It takes work. Some more than others. And the issues that couples face are often areas that the Lord wants us to strengthen, like tolerance, forgiveness, steadfastness, sacrifice."

"So your advice is . . . ?"

"If you love him, hang in there."

"But he cheated on me," she said, hotly. "Not once but twice."

Wendy had always struck the priest as a person who liked things straight, so he didn't mince words. "Are we talking about saving your marriage, or finding a way to salve your wounded pride?"

She thought about that question now as she sat watching Harold slide back into the pew. But even if she could forgive him, would she ever be able to trust him again? No marriage could survive without trust.

George and Ted had finished setting the statue of Saint Anthony in place. She studied its face. Saint Anthony, the saint of miracles, she mused. Her marriage could certainly use one.

"Excuse me, Harold."

"Where are you going?"

"I have to see a saint about a man."

Rodney was the senior altar server today. The mass was being said in thanksgiving for Dexter's miraculous and complete recovery.

His brother was being released from the hospital tomorrow, and although that should have made the boy extremely happy, he also felt a deep pang of remorse, remembering a promise he had made.

Now, looking up at the crucifix behind the altar, he thought, Yep, that's me. I offered to become a priest in exchange for Dexter's life, and God nailed me.

The church was filled to overflowing. Religious affiliation didn't matter. All had come with one heart to share in the wonderment of God's faithfulness.

News about Dexter's incredible recovery had traveled hot and fast, and there wasn't a person in town that didn't want to share in the spirit of thanksgiving for this wondrous renewal of the gift of life.

The Congregationalists were represented by Reverend Curtis and his wife, Emily, and the mayor's family. Colonel Reginald Harris and several members of the Salvation Army were seated behind Saint Cecilia's regulars, Harriet, Ethel, and Arlene. Arlene beamed with pleasure. It was so wonderful to take part again in the mass, something she had not been able to do while Fred was home.

Sam Rosenberg and his rabbi sat together next to the Cliffords, and in front of them, taking up three entire rows, was the Mount Olive Baptist Church choir, their ebony faces shining with God's love. They had come to share their gift of music, which would shake the rafters and give these quiet Catholics a lesson in what it really meant to "make a glad noise unto the Lord."

Honey, who had been a church regular since she was a pup, wound herself into a tight ball on the pew next to her mistress. Ethel smiled into her gentle brown eyes as she stroked the dog's silky fur.

Father James looked out from the altar, noting that Saint Cecilia's head usher, Timothy McGee's, outfit seemed to match the festive mood. He was dressed in a lime green and yellow plaid blazer, orange pants, and a cherry red tie, looking like a bowl of tropical fruit. Ben, more conservatively dressed, stood beside him, ready to help latecomers to their seats.

It was evident by the men's bright cheeks that their spirits were riding high. The footage they had taken of the governor's rescue had been picked up by several major networks, providing them with a nice windfall. Right after mass, the men were going to take Sam and "the girls" on a trip to Atlantic City.

———

Father James prepared to give the homily but when he reached beneath the lectern, he discovered that his notes were missing. Instead, he found a rolled piece of parchment tied with a coarse brown string.

He glanced sheepishly out into the sanctuary. "It seems as though someone has grown tired of my homilies and has replaced my material with this," he announced, laughing and holding up the parchment. Slowly, he unfurled the yellowed paper, whose edges appeared worn with time. He scanned it briefly and then began to smile. It was perfect.

When we walk through the valley, let us not be afraid, because we do not walk alone. As soon as the first prayer is lifted on wings toward God's throne, the Father replies by gathering his forces, including a call to the saints.

In the book of Hebrews, Paul reminds us that we are "surrounded by a great crowd of witnesses that are cheering us on." It is this community of saints that will uphold our petitions before the throne of God.

When we think about the saints, we equate them with our family here on earth. For instance, we might have an uncle who is a great mechanic. Just the person you would call if your car broke down. Or maybe your sister is a gifted seamstress. Wouldn't you contact her if you needed to sew that special dress?

And like our family here on earth, the saints, too, have been endowed with special talents. Saint Frances of Rome is the one you might want to call if you are a widow in need. Or if you're a writer and need help with that article or book, then call upon Saint Francis de Sales.

And let us not confine our pleas for help just to patron saints. Those who we personally have loved and who have died are also a powerful source of intercession.

In second Peter the apostle writes, "And I will make every effort to see that after my departure you will always be able to remember these things."

It follows that for Peter to be aware of our needs, he must be able to look down from heaven and see our struggles, just as your relatives and friends can see your needs and stand ready to intercede on your behalf.

Father James saw Arlene nodding her head in agreement.

But why do we need their prayers? you might ask. Some would say there is no need to circumvent the Lord. Why not go directly to the Father? But we are not circumventing the Lord. We are inviting others to join in our spiritual journey. It's no different from turning to your neighbors right now and asking them to pray on your behalf. Would you consider that circumventing the Father?

Jesus on two separate occasions showed us the powerful intercession of the saints. At the transfiguration, Jesus called upon Moses and Elijah, who discussed events that were about to take place.

On the night before Jesus was betrayed, he pleaded with his disciples to stay awake and pray with him.

My dear brothers and sisters, take solace in the knowledge that you, too, are surrounded by a community of saints, who stand ever ready to offer their prayers on your behalf; to meld their spiritual power with yours so that you may find the strength to "press on toward the goal of your high calling."

Harold helped Wendy on with her coat.

"Aren't you going to put on your gloves?" he asked. "It's kind of cold outside."

"No, I'm fine," she replied, picking up her purse.

"It is awfully cold outside," he repeated. "You should put them on."

She did not want to make an issue of it so she slipped her hand inside her coat pocket for her glove. An envelope was tucked inside.

"Go ahead. Open it," Harold said, with a twinkle in his eye. "Happy Anniversary."

She stared at him dumbfounded. Inside the envelope were tickets for a Bermuda cruise.

"And that's not all. You know how you always hated the fact that I didn't dance. Well, there's a dance band on this cruise, so I decided to surprise you and take lessons. I found a woman over in the next town who gives lessons in her home. Wait until you see me on that dance floor," he said proudly. "I do a *mean* rumba."

Doc Hammon was enjoying his walk through town. The soft scent of violets tinted the air, and a warm gentle breeze portended spring.

It wasn't home cooking that he had missed while a patient, or the comfort of his lounge chair at home, or the smell of clean country air woven in the linens. It was his walks.

He inhaled deeply, the air pure nectar, feeling like Dorothy returned from the land of Oz. *There's no place like home. There's no place like home.*

He often heard patients talk about their travels around the globe, but to be honest, he never felt the need to travel himself. All he held dear could be found right here in Dorsetville—good friends and neighbors; soft, rolling hills; the special beauty of each passing season. No, he thought, heading toward his office, he'd leave traveling the world to others.

It was Saturday and the office was closed, a good time to get things sorted out without all of that confusion and noise.

He let himself in a side door, savoring the familiar scents of disinfectant and Shirley's musky perfume, and headed toward his office at the rear of the suite, peeling off his coat and gloves as he went. He was comforted to discover that his desk had been left undisturbed. It was just as he had left it, stacks of folders and lab reports covering most of it. Shirley must have set up his replacement in another room, he thought, hanging up his coat.

He pulled out the leather desk chair, worn to a soft butter. It had belonged to his dad. Within a few minutes he was fast at work.

Shirley (as efficient as ever) had laid a bright red folder on top of the pile that contained updates on all the patients that Dr. Noiyst had seen in his absence. He removed the first chart from the pile and began to read.

It took him nearly an hour and a half to review everything, including an outbreak of George Benson's hemorrhoids. Doc had told him he should have surgery. George told him he'd rather lose a leg.

All in all, he was very pleased with how Dr. Noiyst had handled things in his absence. Too bad the young physician had left before he could personally thank him. Which reminded him. He should give Morris Leventhal a call and thank him for sending over a replacement . . .

"How'd the surgery go?" Morris asked, seeming a trifle distracted when he answered the phone. It sounded as though there was a party going on in the background.

"Fine. I just came home this morning."

"Sorry for the noise. It's my granddaughter's fifth birthday."

"I won't keep you long, then," Doc said. "I just wanted to thank you for sending Dr. Noiyst to take my place. He did a first-class job. In fact, it's a good thing I got back when I did. A few more weeks and I might have lost most of my practice to that young man."

"Dr. Noiyst?"

"Yes, the young doctor you sent as my replacement while I was away."

"Yes, I remember you called and asked if I knew of someone, but there must be a mistake. I couldn't find anyone. Didn't your receptionist get the fax I sent over?"

"But *someone* sent him."

"It wasn't me." A balloon popped. "Listen, I'm sorry, Jack, but I have to get back to the party. It's time to cut the cake. Glad to hear everything went well with the surgery."

Doc leaned back in his chair. Well, if that didn't beat all. If Morris hadn't sent Dr. Noiyst, then who was the young man who had been taking care of his patients while he was away?

A shaft of light caught something dangling from his desk lamp, and his newly restored heart skipped a beat as he remembered his prayer to his patron saint.

It was a small medal bearing the figure of Saint Anthony of Padua, hung from a thin brown cord of twine.

DISCUSSION QUESTIONS

1. Many people spend a lifetime going from place to place, job to job, seeking to better themselves and find a sense of belonging, yet Doc Hammon has remained in Dorsetville all his life and continues to find delight in his surroundings and friends. What separates Doc from others? Is it just his profession?

2. When Wendy suspects that Harold is cheating, she questions if trust could ever be restored. What element does trust play in a marriage? If trust is broken, can it ever be fully restored?

3. The Bible states that "all things work toward good." What good could come from tragedies, and why would a loving God choose this path as a method of enlightenment?

4. What insights does Dr. Nathan Noiyst's role bring us?

5. Many of those in Dorsetville feel a sudden need to pray for Dexter, unaware of the medical crisis taking place at that moment. Most of us have experienced moments of synchronicity. Have you ever thought of someone out of the blue and later discovered that that person was undergoing a crisis at that particular moment?

6. Women have traditionally been the primary caretakers. Three women—Arlene, Lorraine, and Harvest—have been cast into these roles. How does each role differ? How are they the same?

7. Fred is diagnosed with Alzheimer's and Arlene laments the loss of the memories they shared. What part do memories play in forging relationships?

8. Nothing seems to be going right for George Benson. From time to time, we all experience such pockets of bad luck. Is there anything we can do to effectively turn things around, or must we simply let them run their course? What role, if any, do our thoughts play in attracting these events?

9. What enables some married couples to remain loyal during periods of crisis while other marriages dissolve? Is it the example our parents have provided? Our faith? Societal norms? Consider these questions as they relate to Lorraine and Mike, Wendy and Harold, Harvest and Greg, Arlene and Fred.

10. Father James traces his case of insomnia to his inability to release a roster of concerns—he worries about his parish, his friends, their problems. How often do we take on issues that are clearly outside our ability to resolve them? Is it possible to banish the need to worry, or does it play a role in our development?

© Tracy Studio

Katherine Valentine is the author of three previous Dorsetville novels, *A Miracle for St. Cecilia's* (winner of an honorable mention by the Catholic Press Association), *A Gathering of Angels* (winner of popular presentation of Catholic faith by the Catholic Press Association), and *Grace Will Lead Me Home*. Katherine resides in the New England countryside, where, she says, "Dorsetville lies just outside my front door."